Reclaiming the Vision

Reclaiming the Vision

Past, Present, and Future:

Native Voices for the Eighth Generation

Edited by
Lee Francis (*Laguna Pueblo*)
and
James Bruchac (*Abenaki*)

GREENFIELD REVIEW PRESS

Publication of this volume has been made possible through a Dissemination Grant from the W.K. Kellogg Foundation. *We wish to thank the W.K. Kellogg Foundation and the other funders, in particular* The Bay Foundation *and the* Geraldine R. Dodge Foundation, *for providing generous support for the Returning the Gift Conference which was the genesis for this book.*

ISBN 0-87886-140-8

Library of Congress Number 95-81637

COVER ART by Robert Sisk

Design and Composition
by Sans Serif Typesetters
Ann Arbor, Michigan

Distributed by The Talman Co. Inc.
131 Spring Street
New York, N.Y. 10012
(212) 431-7175 Fax (212) 431-7215

Thank you to all our relations
Those before and those yet to come
Wlidogowgah

—James Bruchac

CONTENTS

INTRODUCTION

Session Four: Earth and the Circle of Life

IN THE CLASSROOM

BEYOND THE CLASSROOM

ANTHOLOGY OF EMERGING NATIVE VOICES

ACKNOWLEDGEMENTS

To Carol Bruchac for all the detail work, Mary Francis for proof-reading, and Sans Serif Inc. for taking on the monumental task of typesetting, our heartfelt thanks.

To W. K. Kellogg . . .

Special thanks to Akwekon Press and the American Indian Program of Cornell University for their assistance in editing and transcribing material from the Returning the Gift Conference.

The Eighth Generation:
Native Writing in the 21st Century

Joseph Bruchac III (Abenaki)

To begin with, none of us were supposed to be here. The idea of manifest destiny was that the American nation which surrounds us all, would stretch from sea to sea and that the identities and the lands of the many original Native nations would be wiped out, extirpated, eliminated, exterminated, rolled over, swallowed, vacuumed up, recycled, remanufactured, or just plain erased by that European-American megalith. The mis-named Indians, those pathetic few who survived, would be assimilated, absorbed like an embarrassing coffee spill soaked up by a Bounty tissue. Their rude languages would be forgotten, their customs preserved only in the dusty volumes of technologists, their only legacy a few mis-told tales, a scattering of misinterpreted and mis-spelled names on the maps of the land, a slightly darker hue in the skins of those who cared or dared to claim that some of their ancestors were Indians.

Adapt and survive. Those are important words for us all. Learn the new language so that you can say your own name and the names of your people. We choose these words, just as we choose to be writers. Garcialosso de la Vega, the Inca, was the first over 400 years ago. *The Florida of the Inca* and the *Royal Commentaries of the Incas*, the history of his own people were the two great volumes written in Spanish by that first modern "American Indian" writer, child of a Spanish nobleman and a Quechun princess of the Inca state. Mixed blood, but he knew who he was and told the stories of his people and this hemisphere.

To adapt is not the same as to assimilate. To survive is to continue. Control of the language, choosing the words that describe your life and the lives of your people, means controlling more of your own destiny, your past, present and future. The circle of your family and your culture.

In the five hundred years since the first recorded arrival of Europeans in the western hemisphere, the lives and destinies of the Native peoples of North America have been affected in many ways. All too often, the "official version" of what happened over that period of five centuries has dis-

xiv   RECLAIMING THE VISION

counted, misrepresented or even totally neglected the original inhabitants
of this hemisphere. Until very recently, few people—aside from Native
people themselves—have been aware of the Native view or of the existence (for several hundred years) of Native literary chroniclers of the
tragedies and triumphs of their own cultures, of their ancient oral traditions, of their experiences of the last five hundred years. Further, though
they have been very much aware of each other, it has not until now been
possible for a substantial number of Native North American writers to
come together, to share and work toward solutions to their common problems, to discuss and celebrate the incredible survival of those who, as Joy
Harjo (*Muscogee*) puts it in one of her poems "were never meant to survive." Nor has the general public been made aware of the scope and the
importance of contemporary Native writing, continent-wide.

The emergence of the work of contemporary Native authors onto the
literary scenes in Canada and the United States has been one of the major
developments in the literature of North America during the past three
decades. It began, most agree, with a Kiowa writer, N. Scott Momaday,
receiving international attention when his novel *House Made of Dawn*
(which takes place primarily on a New Mexico pueblo) won the Pulitzer
Prize for Literature in 1969. Today Momaday's works and books by such
Indian novelists as James Welch (*Blackfeet*), Leslie Silko (*Laguna
Pueblo*), and Gerald Vizenor (*Anishinabe*) are regularly taught in colleges
and ranked with the best of contemporary American fiction.

And the new voices continue to be heard. An anthology I edited in
1983, *Songs From This Earth on Turtle's Back*, contained 52 different Native poets. If I were to do that anthology today, it would contain more than
200. In 1994, *Returning The Gift*, an anthology of work selected from
writers who attended the 1992 festival was published by the University of
Arizona Press, with poetry, prose and drama by 92 writers.

Though publication of drama had lagged behind poetry and fiction,
Hanay Geigomah (*Kiowa*) and William Yellow Robe (*Assiniboine*),
LeAnne Howe (*Choctaw*), Bruce King (*Oneida*), and Spiderwoman Theater (Lisa Mayo, Gloria Miguel and Muriel Miguel, three *Cuna/Rappa-
hannock* sisters) were among the Native playwrights who, by 1992, had
seen their own work frequently produced. The Returning The Gift Festival
spurred the founding in 1993 of the *Native Playwrights Newsletter*, which
has produced half a dozen issues since the festival and provided much information about Native Theater and a continuing forum for the publication of Native plays.

One new development in the last decade has been a surge of energy among the Native writers of Canada, most of whom are still not yet known in the United States. Cherokee novelist Thomas King's fiction anthology *All My Relations* (McClelland Steward, 1990), *Seventh Generation*, an anthology of contemporary Canadian Native poetry edited by Heather Hodgson (Theytus Books, 1989), and *Our Bit of Truth, An Anthology of Canadian Native Literature*, edited by Agnes Grant (Pemmican Publishing, 1990), are three noteworthy and representative anthologies.

Native writers have much in common. Doing interviews with Native writers around the United States (published as *Survival This Way*, University of Arizona, 1987) I discovered that themes of survival and cultural continuance were pervasive and that the dual legacy of English language and Native traditions was widely seen as a tool to serve the community. Though writing is a relatively new thing for Indians (like horses and guns), it can be used for the people in an Indian way. Our literature can play a major role in presenting positive images and alternatives for young Native people—usually often denied such positive models by their schools and the stereotyped images of "Indians" in movies and TV. These challenges remain and will still be with us in the 21st century.

If the ability to write is a gift, then most Native writers seem to agree that it's their responsibility to use that talent for the people, to "return the gift." Although each Native writer is an individual with a special and unique voice, virtually all of these writers are alike in their overall worldview and face similar problems.

The idea of a major gathering of Native writers was in the wind for more than two decades. With that in mind the Returning The Gift project was born with the first National festival in 1992. Returning The Gift was designed to create new opportunities for North American Native writers (fiction and non-fiction writers, poets and playwrights) to share their work and to better educate Native youth, the overall Native community and the general public about contemporary Native literature. This was done through a number of activities, including the formation of not one but several organizations (such as Native Writers Circle of the Americas and Wordcraft Circle of Native Writers and Storytellers), publication of a Directory of North American Native writers, Outreach Programs in Education, and the focal event of a major festival bringing more than 200 Native Writers from all over North America to Norman, Oklahoma from July 8-11, 1992. (It is important to acknowledge that all of this was made possible by generous support from our three primary financial supporters: The

Bay Foundation—which assisted us at every stage, The Geraldine R. Dodge Foundation, and the W. K. Kellogg Foundation.)

Who were the Native writers invited to that festival? The current popularity of Native American writing has resulted not only in many non-Indians jumping on the bandwagon and writing about Native people, but also in some writers who are not Indian passing themselves off as Natives. It's a bit like the resurgence of the old "Medicine Shows" with a crop of pseudo-shamans feeding on New Age needs by selling sweat lodges and vision quests. Therefore, in defining who is a "Native writer" we suggested these guidelines (genetic, cultural, and social) used by Geary Hobson (*Cherokee-Quapaw/Chickasaw*) for inclusion in his anthology *The Remembered Earth*: a Native writer is a writer who has provable Native ancestry (American Indian, Eskimo, Aleut), who defined himself or herself as a Native writer and is accepted by the community to which they claim to belong, with the Indian tribe or community's judgement being of utmost importance. Both established writers and writers at the start of their careers were to be invited, with all of their expenses paid and with a modest honorarium paid to those more established writers who would act as mentors.

Since that festival in 1992, by my latest count, more than 60 books have been published by writers who attended. More then half of them had no book in print prior to the Returning The Gift Festival. Many of those books were a direct result of contacts made at the festival.

Things will continue to be more complicated—or more interesting—in this eighth generation. We'll still have that familiar argument about who is and isn't Indian. It is an argument that usually looks at a very brief span of time and forgets seven generations. An impatient argument which tried to settle something quickly that may take centuries to sort out. We've had 500 years and more of it so far. Maybe it will take another 500. That isn't that long. We need a long view and a long memory and we need to remember we're on a circle, not a straight line or a graph with a population curve on it. The argument of who is and who isn't Indian is an argument that can once again divide us, now that we are starting once more to grow strong. It is an argument which conveniently forgets the complexities of the histories and traditions of hundreds of different nations by jumbling them all together. BIA or unenrolled, full blood or mixed blood? Real, semi-real, marginal, phony? And what about those multi-ethnic Indians, those who are Cuna/Rappahannock or Tlingit/Lakota or

Hopi/Navajo/Pueblo/Apache? And what about their kids who, though "pure Indian" may end up being 1/16 of 16 different tribes?

When I talk about this I think I hear our ancestors laughing. Not only at the audacity of the federal government to say who is and who isn't really Indian, but at the narrowness of definitions and the reasons for making those definitions. Our ancestors know who they were and they know how the balance will affect us. And what, they might say, do you new folks call those of us who aren't even descended from human beings? What about those of us who are Abenakis and say that some of our people were turned into water animals and fish in a big flood and that every now and then one of those real mixed-bloods comes back on land and marries a human being? What about those folks who know that one of their fairly recent ancestors was a bear? Was it your mother's or father's side, the census taker asks. If you are more than 1/4 Ursus Horribilis then you cannot be enrolled as an Indian. Is it easier to accept adopting a bear as an ancestor and still think of yourself as an Indian than it is to have a white person back there and still be a skin?

In the 21st Century, the job of the Native writer will continue to be a simple one, despite all these complexities. It will be to follow the hard road of writing, to follow it despite anger and sorrow, despite loss and pain, to write out of the spirit and the memory, to write out of the turmoil and the possibility, to know your heart and the heart of your people, to stand in that place and to write. It is a good time today to be young, to be Native and to be alive. May many more generations continue to follow the word trail.

RETURNING THE GIFT
PLENARY SESSIONS

CELEBRATING THE VISION

Lee Francis (*Laguna Pueblo*)

"I didn't know there were so many Indian writers' repeated the 16-year-old Choctaw high school student from northern California. It was difficult to hear what the young Native writer was saying in the packed, noisy, smoke-filled restaurant.

He and I and at least thirty other Native writers and storytellers were all sitting at a patch-work of small tables shoved together to make a large one. It seemed like the blond haired student was doing his best to act nonchalant about the whole affair. "Don't let it bother you, we're all just folks" I said in voice that sliced through most of the noise from dozens of conversations.

He told me he was one of the high school and college students invited to attend the Returning The Gift Festival and that this was the first time he had ever been to Oklahoma. As we continued our disjointed conversation, I could see that he was overwhelmed by all the prominent Native writers and storytellers carrying on lively conversations with long-time colleagues they hadn't seen in months or years.

I understood. To see so many beginning, emerging and established Native writers and storytellers participating in the Festival being held at the University of Oklahoma in Norman was amazing. I was also caught up in the excitement of finally getting to meet a number of Native writers whose work I had read and admired over the years.

Responding to the young Choctaw's question, I told him about my work with Native students across the country for over a decade. I said that I was especially looking forward to meeting and getting to know the Native high school and college students attending the Festival. He smiled self-consciously when I said that "seeing the world from a Native student's perspective always inspires me . . . especially when I'm writing."

In the course of our conversation, I explained that I wanted to be able to tell students I work with across Indian Country what their peers experienced during the four-day event. We visited for awhile and then the young Choctaw high school student decided to leave. An hour or so later, I left the restaurant and went to my room and was asleep minutes after going to bed.

The Festival began the next morning with breakfast in the dining hall. There were at least 150 Festival participants standing in line or already sitting and eating their breakfast. I wasn't ready for all those people. I got some coffee and sat at an empty table. After a few minutes, the young Choctaw high school student I had met the night before waved at me from another table. I wondered briefly if he was still being nonchalant.

After drinking several cups of coffee, I joined the crowd walking to the auditorium building next to the dining hall for the Opening Ceremonies. As my eyes adjusted from the glare of the bright morning sun to the relative darkness of the auditorium, I looked around and laughed when I saw my own disbelief reflected in the eyes of others who were equally surprised to see so many Native writers and storytellers taking their seats.

Joseph Bruchac III (*Abenaki*), the Chairman of the Returning The Gift Steering Committee, called the Festival to order and introduced the organizers of the gathering. For Joe, after more than three years of planning the event, the moment had finally arrived. It was Joe who began the whole process by contacting other well-established and esteemed Native writers and storytellers about holding a conference and gently suggesting that it be called Returning The Gift. From where I sat, it seemed as if sheer joy radiated from him at seeing so many Native writers and storytellers in the audience for the opening session.

After the introductions, Ted Williams (*Tuscarora*) asked blessings from the Creator. It seemed that most of the Festival participants understood the significance of the prayer leader being of a sovereign nation from the eastern area of Indian Country. For Native people of the sovereign nations and tribes, East is the place of beginnings. It is where the light of the sun first touches Indian Country.

Following the Invocation, Eddie Wilson, Chairman of the Cheyenne-Arapaho Nation, welcomed us to The Indian Territory. Being greeted and welcomed by a member of a sovereign Nation to the current homeland of that Nation was also significant.

As I studied the Festival schedule, it was clear that the organizers were also deeply committed to meeting the needs of our younger relations.

The Plenary Session for the first day was titled: "Writing for Our

Children, Writing for Ourselves—Native Writing and Native Identity." The second day of the conference, the Plenary Session's focus was "Emerging Native Images—Natives in the Media—Books and Texts." The third day's Plenary Session was titled, "Entering the Canons—Our Place in World Literature." On the fourth and final day of the Festival, the Plenary Session focused on "Earth and the Circle of Life—Native Writers and the Environment." Selected talks from the four morning Plenary Sessions and the afternoon workshops are presented in this first section of the book.

What was even more exciting for me were the Student Readings scheduled all four days of the Festival. The students were astounding. They read their writings like old pros. Speaking from their hearts, the students captured and held the attention of even the most cynical. They had important thoughts and feelings to tell us and we listened with growing admiration.

The ferocious intensity the high school and college students displayed when talking about their writing experiences fascinated me. I remember thinking at one point that if I had been as zealous about writing at their age, I would have been awarded at least three Pulitzer prizes by the time I was 40. They understood the value of writing. At times I would laugh and remind these new warriors, fully armed with their sacred word-bundles, that they didn't have to convince me because we were in the same choir.

"Writing is important for everything you do in life," I overheard one student pronounce to the Native novelist who had written and published more than 20 books in a five year period. It took me a moment to realize that the student had no idea who the Native novelist was much less his noteworthy accomplishments. "Ah, the student teaches the elder" I murmured to no one in particular. I looked at the accomplished novelist and noticed the beginnings of a smile. A gentle man, I thought and before I had the chance to quietly wander into the conversation, a high school student glided up to me and asked, "Did you like my story?"

I turned and looked at her. "Yes. I liked your story very much." Her eyes glowed with pride as she began to explain why she had written it. It seemed like she wanted something from me, but I couldn't figure out what it might be. "Why do you think writing is important?" was all I could think to ask to keep the conversation going.

"I don't know." she responded hesitantly. "I guess for me it's important because I want to tell stories so I can express my feelings through my characters."

"Do you think there is any value in writing stories?" I asked, wanting to hear more about what she thought and felt.

"Value? I don't know what you mean."

"Well, you said that writing stories was important because you were able to express your feelings. I was wondering if expressing your feelings was the only reason for your writing."

"Oh. I don't know. I guess writing is an outlet for me. It helps me understand myself and the world." She paused for an instant and I watched a frown ripple across her face. "I think writing is important because, for me, it's a way to tell others my ideas and feelings and hopefully make a better world for all of us."

The following selections are excerpts from the talks given in the plenary sessions of the Returning The Gift Festival. The selections are not word-for-word transcriptions because extemporaneous speaking does not lend itself to clear communication when transferred to paper. And while the major points of each talk are faithfully presented, in some instances extensive editing was done to emphasize the speaker's key message.

SESSION ONE
WRITING FOR OUR CHILDREN,
WRITING FOR OURSELVES

Native Writing and Native Identity

Leslie Marmon Silko (*Laguna Pueblo*)

No, the Indian didn't die. The Indians don't die. And we get our land back. That's going to happen, that's coming.

What I first would like to talk about today is how we have been, as Native American people and tribal people in the United States, cut off from other Native peoples in the Americas and also across the world. Telling us to ignore the tribal people in Canada and to forget about the people in Mexico, which is what the United States government is always doing, is a way, in my view, of getting ready to send tribal Native people out to kill other tribal Native people around the world.

So, we've got to try to break away from the notion that we are just United States citizens and understand that we are internationally sovereign nations. And while we love this land, and know that this land is our land, it is the government that calls the shots and draws the boundaries. What we need to do is to forget about international boundaries which have been set up, in my view, to perpetuate exploitation, genocide, and ultimately the destruction of the world. We've got to see that we belong to the world. We have a worldwide role—we always have—which joins us together with other tribal people who are still close to the earth. If all of us and all living things on the planet are to continue, we, who still remember how we must live, must join together.

What I also want to talk about is translators and translations. One of the things that we need to do at the same time we work on our Native languages and writing to our people is to make an effort to reach out. We've got to see more translations from Spanish into English, from our brothers and sisters to the South. We also have to remember the African tribal people. There is an ancient, ancient tie between West African and the Caribbean people. Spiritual ties. Religious ties. We cannot forget that it all fits together, and we can't be cut off.

I want to emphasize that in terms of our self-image we've got to see that this is the beginning, and we have to become active and involved. So, translators, it's very important that our work be translated, and writings in Spanish come to English. It is also important that we work with the translators in European languages because for so long we've been cut out of the world community.

I really feel that the most important thing we can do is to disregard those boundaries that have been drawn and reach out. This is the renaissance. This is the beginning, and in order to make sure that this continues, it is important that we see ourselves as citizens of the world. That's all I want to say. Thank you very much.

Storytelling

A. C. "Chuck" Ross (*Lakota*)

I'm from South Dakota. I live on Pine Ridge reservation in a village called Kyle, which is on southern edge of the Badlands. When I first moved there, my friend Doug asked, "what's that about Kyle. What's them Badlands like?"

I said, "Well, it's buttes and canyons. There's nothing to live off of there. Just snakes, lizards, and a lot of box canyons. As a matter of fact, during the 1930s there were some cows that fell down one of those canyons and got trapped in there. They started to inbreed and in the 1940s this herd of cattle was discovered down there in that box canyon. They were all three foot high because they had inbred that long. They brought them out and put the miniature cattle in traveling shows."

So Doug says to me that he went to the carnival where he saw a miniature horse that was two foot six inches high.

I said, "Well, you know when I was stationed in Germany, they have miniature deer over there called red deer that are only eighteen inches high."

Doug thought for awhile and then he said that he had gone to a circus where he'd seen a monkey ten inches high. It was called a spider monkey I think. I said to Doug, "You win. I don't have a story that can top that one!"

Telling stories—handing down our legends—is our tradition, not only among Lakota people but all Indian people.

When I was young, I thought that the way you got all your knowledge and information was by reading. Then, when I came back from Europe, I started visiting with my grandparents and I realized there was a whole wealth of knowledge there. I did not document my visits. I didn't use a tape recorder or go around with paper and pencil. The reason for that is because back home we have been studied to death.

So when I visited with elders and grandparents, I just tried to remember as much as I could. Later, I dictated what I remembered onto a tape in storytelling fashion. I hired a stenographer to type it up and then I went through the manuscript and corrected it for language. After all that had been done, I submitted the manuscript to an editor. In short, it was a long, tedious process.

As I was writing the book, I was afraid Indian people would be upset about writing down our oral history. You've heard the old phrase that Indians are like a bucket of crabs? In my opinion, that saying comes from the fact that we are tribal people, we're group oriented. And because we are tribal people, the minute you become an "I," then you're an outsider. As a result, the group will ridicule and/or ostracize you to try to get you back into the group.

After I finished the book, I have not had one complaint about writing down the oral history. Matter of fact, the book is now being used in twenty-seven universities along with the teacher's guide we developed. So with that, I'll end my talk. Thank you.

Vi Hilbert (*Upper Skagit*)

For a long time I resisted putting our stories into books. In fact, I was discouraged from doing it for a long, long time. But I'm an only child and because I am now a great-grandmother, I have a responsibility.

In my view, it is important for the world to hear our languages. Our ancestors left those languages for our spirits to identify with, and we think things best in our own languages. This is why I have been collecting all the stories I can from the culture of my people since 1967, so that future generations may benefit from their wisdom—and wisdom it is—that can be shared with the entire world. Some of it is private and will not be shared. However, most of it can be shared because the stories apply to human nature around the world.

It is also important for each of us to realize that there is a commonality to the way every ancestor in our world taught their young people using traditional stories. These stories are the original textbooks to teach our young people.

So, in order to teach the language, the literature and the culture through traditional stories, I had to create my own books so that I would have something from which to teach. In creating my own books, I listened to the stories, the histories, the songs, that were told by my relatives. Also, there was important information which had been tape recorded in the early 1930s and was available for me to listen to. As I listened to the scratchy recordings, I wrote down every word that was spoken. In understanding what was said, I could then try to find words in the English language to properly translate what these beautiful people were leaving for our young people. The stories are beautiful and told in the language of my people.

Because there was a great need in the communities all over the Puget Sound area for the stories, I transferred them to written form. Then, when I began teaching at the University of Washington, I first taught the language and later incorporated the literature in the language.

The students I taught heard the stories from the original storyteller who had a way of expressing what he or she saw graphically in the language. They learned the important way the original storytellers had of drawing a picture for you of what that story meant. For example, the storyteller might use the symbolism, or metaphor, or even the voices of many characters that were animals, who were really people in my culture. These are the things that the original storytellers were able to impart to us.

When I write a story, I can't do that. Which is why I'd rather tell a story and then let people read it after they have heard me tell it. That, to me, is the best way. Let's write our stories, and also, let us tell them, so young people can hear the way we tell them. That is what I think is important.

Poetry Writing

Eleanor Sioui (*Huron/Wyandot*)

I started writing poetry after I discovered that there was more than one way to do it. With poetry we can make sounds in all kinds of ways that will affect and enhance feeling just as an amplifier or a speaker enhances the voice. Poetry is supposed to do that. It is intended that our bodies will feel the vibrations and the rhythms. You can use the rhythms, you can hear the rhythms, but I recommend to you to read poetry from other countries. Listen to different kinds of rhythms and a different kind of arrangement.

For those who know your language, notice that in our songs we don't rhyme in most of our Indian languages. Our songs are based on a beat. There are repeat lines and choruses. You say a chorus line or even one word and it stops a thought. That's a pattern that gives an image. You can recognize that pattern if you are listening to those sounds that enhance.

I think the best technical thing you can use with poetry is to use your heart. What hurts you, what makes you cry? What makes you feel afraid, what makes you sad? What comes in your mind when I say lost? Is there a toy or a doll that you lost? What did you lose? Think of some ways you can tell what it meant to lose that?

Political experience is also important. To get people to stop polluting the stream, you may need to dig and use your dead dog. Use the sorrow in your heart that is real, like the sorrow of a child for a death or a loss of some kind, and use that sorrow to describe the way you feel now, not your head, but your feelings.

In poetry, we sometimes use our education. I think of the words for something enormous, humongous, huge, colossal It's big! Big loss! Something that flattens you out. You don't want to say, "I was devastated." Instead you want to say, it flattened me. The word that's closest to the heart of a child, the word that kicks you in your stomach. That word is the word that you want. That is what is called genuine voice.

A genuine voice is a way that you write—this is the way I do it. This is the voice of my heart, that is what I want to say, this is the way I want to say it. And when you do that, it's not like anybody else's. It's very different. Poets make their statements through genuine voice, genuine style. It's the way you speak when you are your best self.

If I was going to recommend something to you, it would be to listen to the childhood voice. Do you remember stories you were told as a kid? What were you doing when they were telling it to you? Where were you sitting? Was there a dog? Was there a bird? What did it sound like? Were you sitting on the porch on the rough boards? In summary, put the five senses in when writing poetry. Then tell a story. It will be about you sitting there on the porch, on the rough boards, listening to the birds. That will be what you should tell when writing poetry.

Writing in Native Languages

Ofelia Zepeda (*Tohono O'odham*)

My background is in linguistics and American Indian studies. I started out writing poetry as sort of a hobby. The unusual thing about it is that I began writing in my native language.

As a linguist, I'm also an educator. I do what they call teacher training. In the years that I've been working as an educator of potential teachers, it has been my goal to make a change, and I hope I am beginning to, along with other people who have been doing similar things in recent years.

The change I am referring to is about the young people, the children, and the image they have of themselves, which certainly says something about the image that we have of ourselves. What I know is that, as Native people, we have almost always in common our sense of identity, which is closely related to that essence that we want to call space, or place, which is basically the land. In much of the writing by Native writers out there, that our young people are reading, this is what it is telling them.

As a linguist I have worked in offering courses in American Indian linguistics and creative writing. There is no greater pleasure than to have one of your students who is a teacher, or a teacher aide, come back to you with one of their students' writing. In that sort of circle many of us have seen where the educational process has gone the full circle of affecting teachers, who affect students, who then come back to you and of course, contribute to the wider field of American Indian literature.

As an educator and as a trainer of teachers, it is my philosophy that in order for any of us, no matter what tribe, to maintain a pool of singers, a pool of dancers, a pool of dreamers, star gazers, poets, writers, essayists, whatever, there needs to be those models, not only models as people, but certainly the model of the text being there for them, and instilling that in these young writers. I have been very fortunate to see this circle take place.

My emphasis in working with Native American languages gives me a pragmatic edge in that there is imminent danger of language loss. Educators and tribal people look towards writing and other creative activities in the Native language as a way of maintaining, restoring, or reviving that language.

Harold Littlebird (*Laguna/Santo Domingo Pueblo*)

Some of us didn't grow up on the reservation like I did, so they haven't had the opportunity to understand their languages first hand. So we look for places where we can still hold onto the identity of who we are as a people and that we come from a place.

It is through the written languages we know that we can still hold onto those things because we know we all come from story. We know we all come from places of emergence. They may not all be the same story but there is a sameness. There is a oneness in it all and it comes from language. It comes from places where the word was sacred, and is sacred, and will remain sacred.

Our responsibility as writers is to keep that sacredness alive with story, with songs, with our legends, with our myths, to instill this into our own children so that they begin to have a sense of well-being and wholeness in terms of from where creative power comes. To feel the interconnectedness with all things doesn't just come from word. It comes from that further place of thought, where we take thought and put it into language. In that process we begin to understand what it is that our people have held onto, with language, with their ceremonies, with their prayers and their meditations, and the songs, and the dances, and the rituals. We understand how we as people have to hold onto that, whether it's in the same language that our great grandfathers and grandmothers knew, or in a language that we come up with as writers.

As a writer, I have tried to take word to a different place, with music, because music seems to have a way of reaching a different audience, and giving a creative spirit to it. When we begin to do this, then our children find a place they can identify with themselves. They get a sense of self-centeredness, self-awareness. They begin to hold onto these things, the same way that we want to hold onto these things.

Also important for me as a writer, as a poet, as a songwriter, but above all as a human being, in whatever way I involve myself in being creative or sharing that creativity, there's always the asking, saying help me. That's one thing that we forget sometimes, in our own arrogance as human beings. We forget that we have to ask. When we forget that then we put ourselves in a place of saying we're better than something, and we're not. We're just one part of it.

There are visual reminders out there all the time, and then there's all the spirits around us that help us remember these things. So we have to accept that responsibility and we have to honor it. It's through whatever we do physically as human beings to help one another remember these things, that's where the real responsibility comes in.

I think that's what's important about the stories we create as writers. It's something that helps someone to be reminded, and to help hold onto a way of remembering. Remembering who we are and where we come from. Thank you.

SESSION TWO
EMERGING NATIVE IMAGES

Weaving Together Our Community Voice

Beth Brant (*Bay of Quinte Mohawk*)

I've wanted to talk about communities, and not just one community. I feel that I am a part of so many communities—the Indian community, the Mohawk community, working class community, the gay and lesbian community. The feminist community.

I am part of the community of human people, and bird people and animal people and fish people, and the green people, and the rock people. Bringing all those parts of myself into writing is what I would call integrity, and I think in the twentieth and twenty-first century, these emerging Native images are coming from many different communities, merging, blending, weaving together. It's not an individualistic voice, it's a community voice. I find this very wonderful, because at the same time that I am writing from these many communities, I am being fed by these communities. I'm fifty-one, and I started writing when I was forty, and it was a gift that was given to me. It's a great responsibility, but it's one that I welcome.

I was raised by my Mohawk grandparents, Maggie and Joseph Brant. My grandmother did not speak the Mohawk language that much but my grandfather spoke it every day and he taught me the Mohawk language. That was a gift. For me, the gift of language is the gift of culture. I hear people speaking in their own languages. The multi-lingual poetry and prose is so incredibly moving and beautiful.

So my grandad gave me the gift of language. My Daddy gave me so many gifts. My Daddy was a scholar whose name will never be on books or in institutions of learning, but he knew so much about the history of Indian people and he taught me that. I feel part of being a writer is returning that gift, not just back to him, but to my grandsons. I'm a grandmother now. I have three glorious grandsons, and I feel being a writer is also about writing for them too.

I think a lot of Native writing takes place in the past and future. The present is sort of like a nebulous, almost an unreal place. It's the past and future, and making those into something viable for our communities, for our children, our grandchildren. As writers, we are also resisters and freedom fighters. That word, freedom fighters, is not used anymore. I know it was quite popular during the sixties, but I still like that word, because that is what we're doing, we're fighting for freedom to be who we are.

The way we are writing about ourselves and our communities is so very beautiful. There's always this idea that you want to take the words and you want to make them into something of lasting beauty, like beaded earrings or turquoise and silver, something that will last that will be beautiful. I find that Native writing is like that—a lasting, beautiful thing. I'm very encouraged by the fact that there are young people who are writing. Writing beautifully. Writing lasting beauty. I think that's what Native writing is. We're keeping the drum playing. Niaweh.

Natives in the Media

Alex Jacobs/Karoniaktatie (*Mohawk*)

We have to support the emerging young people coming out now. That's what we have to do. We have to support our own press, our own media. We have to create our own radio stations, our own TV stations.

We have to get together and create programs for radio and TV. The TV and radio station owners are not going to come to you. You have to go to them. You have to demand. You have to request. You have to do anything you can to get on the airwaves, get your voice on the airwaves, get your language on the airwaves.

Then, your neighbors will be hearing you talk. They listen to us. They'll come to us for news. They're not going to go to the networks. They will end up listening to what you have to say. They will hear how we talk about our children, how we talk to our elders. Native people will be listening to us.

Native radio has taken off, and there are dozens and dozens of stations popping up across the country. In Canada, I think there are two hundred Indian radio stations alone in Quebec.

That potential, that future, is what we're looking at as writers. That's nothing against books. We'll always be making books for the children, but our children are already tapped into radio and TV. That's where they're at. We have to go out to where Indian people and Indian kids can see what we're doing with words and images.

We also have to support the technical people such as Indian lawyers, engineers and technicians. As writers, we are the creative side. And while there is a creative, intuitive thing about Indian people, we have to support our technicians too. We have to somehow connect with them. There should be more collaborations between the creative Indian people and the Indian technicians and engineers. We have to maintain a relationship with them.

The same is true for the bookmakers, booksellers, bookpushers. They should also be active and involved. Don't just promote their books or push their books. They have to be involved with the kids in the schools.

It's not just words, it's the actions. It's not just theory. It's not just how creative you can be about imagining to be an Indian. You have to make that connection with your people and your communities.

Autobiographical Writing

Nora Dauenhauer (*Tlingit*)

I belong to a clan, and I belong to a house, and all of these are my identity. Each Native person has an identity similar to mine, but there are differences. I have to keep this in mind, that somebody has an identity, similar to mine, but a little bit different than mine.

I do the research in the field and I work with the elders. I write the stories in Tlingit then translate them into English. It's a lot of work. It's very tedious and very hard because our children and those under the age of forty do not speak the language. In fact, there are about four people who are Tlingit that speak the Tlingit language who are forty and a little over forty. Because there are so few who speak the Tlingit language, we have to do this for the sixteen thousand or less Tlingit people. There's nobody else doing it now.

I want to talk about the elders and some conflicting ideas about oral literature. The idea was not to document, or when to document, or why we should document. I think with a language that's dying, we have to consider what we have to do right now. The elders think documenting the language is a good idea. There's no conflict in their mind that this should or should not be done.

And although it creates a lot of conflict within me, the idea to write it down always wins out. The way I do it is to take the transcriptions to the people who are the givers of the story or oratory. I read it to them to make sure everything they want included is in it and everything they want excluded is out of it. So in this way, there is nothing that doesn't belong.

Robert Perea (*Oglala Lakota*)

I've been writing for about twenty years and it's taken me all this time to finally get a book published. I got lucky and won the short fiction award, so the book is going to be published. Mostly what I write about is the Vietnam War and it is very autobiographical. I teach at Central Arizona College, and whenever I read stories about Vietnam, the first thing the students ask me is, did that really happen? Were you really there? Of course, when you write fiction, everything isn't verbatim, but it's based on things that really did happen.

What I write about is autobiographical because it's from my own experience and sometimes the word fiction kind of bothers me because it is more real than fiction. Lately, I've been writing stories where I haven't even changed the names of the characters. I recently wrote about a cousin of mine, and I used his real name. I wrote a short story about my grandmother, and I used her name. I'm thinking about writing a short story about my niece who my sister adopted, and using her name. Basically, everything I write is very personal.

Another thing I want to talk about are some autobiographies about Vietnam that I have been reading. I came across one that's about the hunter-killer teams they had during the Vietnam war. The hunter-killer teams were helicopters. One was a low flying helicopter that would fly over the Vietcong, and the Vietcong would shoot, and then another helicopter above it would swoop down after the Vietcong started shooting. I got the book because the author was at the same place, at the same time I was; sort of a coincidence.

The thing that's bothered me about that book though, is that it tells all the facts, but it doesn't really get into any of the turmoil, any of the emotion, any of the real heart and soul of the Vietnam way, which is what I am really interested in.

The author has almost a John Wayne attitude. He gets in this helicopter, rides around, finds some VC, shoots them, even calls them the bad guys, then flies back to base camp, has a few beers, then does it again the next day. This is an autobiography, but I was disappointed because there's not any sense of, like I say, "what the hell were we doing over there."

I think my short stories are more autobiographical and more real about how I felt than this book, which is considered an autobiography. That's really all I have to say.

A. C. "Chuck" Ross (*Lakota*)

I wrote an autobiography for several reasons. Maybe the primary reason I wrote the autobiography is because my first book was being reviewed by Hollywood producers and one producer from HBO, for a possible movie. I discussed that with my agent; what the possibilities might be to make a movie out of it. He said a number of things. They are looking at how they can market it; if it will sell. One guy made a joke and asked if it had any sex or violence. It doesn't. There's no storyline in this book. One the reader stated that it would make an excellent movie if it had a storyline. So that was the impetus to start an autobiography.

I sat down and thought about an autobiography. I talked with my wife about it who asked "are we going to reveal our whole lives to everybody?" She was against it because she said "autobiographies are written by elders. We're too young!"

For me, an autobiography is a way of taking a look at oneself. Taking a look at your weaknesses and admit that you have weaknesses and then go about straightening yourself out. So, in the book, I'm an alcoholic. I drank for twenty-two years. Now, I've been sober for seventeen. That's a story I wanted to make sure was in my book, so my children and other people's children could benefit. Also, in the book, I was a male chauvinist pig, and I had to admit that.

Those are some of the reasons why I wrote the book. I'm not really a writer. I'm an educator by profession. When I was growing up, one teacher tried to make me right-handed. I had a natural inclination to the left. But as a result, I never really developed either side, and I cannot write in cursive. Even today, I still cannot write, I just print. So it's very difficult for me to sit down with thoughts buzzing through my head. I can't keep up with it. I also have two thumbs when it comes to typing. So, the way it worked for me was to dictate my message and then hire a stenographer to type it for me. Then I went through and corrected it. That's what worked for me. That's how I wrote autobiography of my life. That's what brought me here.

Teaching Native American Literature

Carroll Arnett/Gogisgi (*Cherokee*)

Since 1970, I've taught at Central Michigan University in Mt. Pleasant, Michigan. Until maybe 1974, my experience at CMU had been a very traditional one, just teaching freshman composition, reading and writing courses. In large part, because of the impetus given to Indian issues and Indian concerns in the early seventies, I got the bright idea of teaching an Indian literature course. I'd been reading Indian literature for a number of years. Now, I proposed it as a special topics course, and lo and behold, it was accepted. At first, the course was offered every year. Then, as Indians became less popular in the late seventies it's offered only every other year.

The course, as I originally conceived it, hasn't changed a great deal since its inception in the seventies. I changed the titles of some of the books. As far back as I can remember, Momaday's *House Made of Dawn* has been a standard item on the book list

The vast majority of students in the class these days are non-Indian people who, if they know anything about Indian culture at all, have picked it up in bits and pieces; maybe in an Anthropology course they had earlier. Because of that innocence on the part of the students, I've ordinarily found myself spending the first four weeks doing an introduction to traditional Indian culture, so they'll have a basic framework.

I start with Pre-Columbian work, songs, chants, old myths and stories, and then move to the nineteenth century. I inevitably use *"Black Elk Speaks,"* one of the classics. One of my very favorite books, and one I think I've had considerable success with in the course, has been the biography of Crazy Horse by Marie Sandoz. I don't want to slight the old work, the old stories—you have to have that—but I'm always eager to get to the twentieth century because the writing is much more exciting. About mid-semester, after doing some work with the nineteenth century and before, I get into the contemporary work. We use Geary Hobson's *"The Remembered Earth,"* plus such novels as Leslie Silko's *"Ceremony,"* Scott

Momaday's *"House Made of Dawn,"* and James Welch's *"Winter in the Blood."*

I've had a dream, from the time I came to CMU, of establishing a Native Studies program, but the dream has been stymied by administrative stupidity. I remember the first time I approached the dean about doing some initial-stage work towards a full-fledged Native Studies program. He said, "Well, that's very interesting. How many students can you guarantee me?" I said, "I can't guarantee any students until I have a program going." So it's a Catch-22 situation. You can't get the program until you get the students, you can't get the students until you get the program, and that's been very, very frustrating.

Carter Revard (*Osage*)

The place where I teach, Washington University in St. Louis, Missouri, was founded by T. S. Eliot's grandfather. It's a private school, which means that it costs like hell and the students all want to believe that they're at Harvard. You get a lot of nice, really decent, good, intelligent students trying to do good things there. But when the Wounded Knee confrontation happened, everybody said we better do something about this. They pointed to me and basically said, "Gee, you've got some Indian background, let's see what you can do."

So when I started teaching these things in 1973 and 1974, I had to scrounge around because it was a little hard to put together current writings for the courses. I also felt I had to read everything I could. For example, if I was going to teach something about Geronimo, I had to read everything I could on the Apache—to learn all that people tell you—and I didn't have many Apache people I could talk to there.

What I'm trying to say is that the literature and the teaching of that literature I don't think of as just creating a literature course. I didn't think of the literature as just "here are these words on the page that I'm teaching in class." I thought of it as coming from the People all over the country who are trying to say *we're here.*

So, what I tried to do was develop a course in which I went from the ceremonial into the personal, if you could call it that, but still creating ceremony. When I came to the modern time, I also taught some Welch novels, some Silko novels, and some Erdrich novels. And the poetry I talked about varied a lot more. I try to teach Wendy Rose every time I get a chance because I think she's one of the great poets. The structure of the course as it has evolved is a way of getting the ceremonial through the personal, still ceremonial, into current novels.

I'm trying to give you the sense that I'm in a traditional English department in some ways. My course is taught as an English course, as a topics course. I have a wide list of books and a lot of freedom to choose. When I teach Indian literature—sometimes I teach it in the other courses and when I sneak it in—I don't believe it just teaches Indian literature, I believe it teaches about American and European people. That's how I see it.

Denise Sweet (*White Earth Anishinabe*)

I would like to talk about a method of working primarily with non-Indian students. I teach at the University of Wisconsin at Green Bay, which is just down the road apiece from Oneida, Wisconsin.

At UW, students are required to take a course that has some multicultural emphasis, some diversity approach in it, and most times, students will opt to take the Indian literature course. The first week we address where they're coming from. I don't hold the students responsible for what they've learned or not learned in the educational system. I want them to know that I come from that system too. What we try to do that first week is address the stereotypes, how they came to be, and really try to understand what the sources are.

I also want them to know that we come from a place that springs forth from story. Native people know that, and a lot of people believe in that, but what does that mean? I guess for my students, non-Indian students in particular, it means that they also have an oral tradition. They have their creation accounts, they have their traditional dances, they have their own secular narratives. One of my basic requirements is that they get in touch with their own oral tradition and then come to my classroom and tell a story.

What we do is use the format of the talking circle. They learn what it means to be equal, to be respected, to be honored as people who have words that are important. For me, one of the most important lessons for them to understand is that our oral tradition is an important focus from which springs the written word. That's our inspiration. It's the view that gives itself away through the story, and I think it makes a difference in my classes.

Most of the time, what I want to do with the written work is to create new themes. I use some of the "greatest hits" from Indian literature, and most of the time I try to work with contemporary literature because it helps me address some of the stereotypes as well. When you come fresh to *Love Medicine*, for example, lots of the students react to the poverty and the anguish, the pain, the drinking, the promiscuity, and on and on. So we talk about that. I help them adjust their world view in some way that allows for a value system that is different. I tell them to not be afraid about that and not to treat Native people as though we're continually and endlessly offended by white people.

One of the things I hope I leave my students with is the understanding that our literature used to be about our dilemma with the white man. Now, it's about the struggles we have that are tribal, that are within our community, the politics which are individual struggles that are of human concern. These are the struggles of all people to maintain an integrity, to maintain autonomy within a society that would seek to oppress them. It's about plain old survival, and both the pain and the beauty in that. When my students leave, I hope they get that message.

SESSION THREE
ENTERING THE CANONS

Our Place in World Literature

Lance Henson (*Cheyenne*)

I would like to begin my comments today by talking about a question that I've been asking myself since I got here, and that's why am I here? Why did I come to this place? I think that question is a mirror that you should be looking at also.

For five hundred years, indigenous people on this planet have suffered under the thumb of oppressing governments. Our literature has also been suppressed. In this country, maybe every ten or twelve years, an Indian writer is allowed to make it. Some of you are sitting here now. The harsh reality of being an indigenous person is upon us. We are representative voices of our people. That doesn't put us in front of them. It puts us at the heart of them.

I would like to share with you the prophecy of the Cheyenne. Sweet Medicine was a young man who was born into our people some years ago, and he gave us the laws that we Cheyenne people try to follow. This is what he told us about our future. He said that it would be a difficult task to try to live in this life, because we would always be outnumbered. We would have to be accepting of other people and other people's ways. Sweet Medicine also said that there would come a time when the caring people of the world would gather because they knew their childrens' futures were in peril. That's why I say that we have to make our voices important to ourselves because the dominant society does not want to hear those voices. We have to make our literature reflect the true reality of being tribal people.

Indian reality is not time-based. We are living in history present all the time and that's very important. Indigenous people on this planet are the few people who still live in those ways. That allows us the opportunity to see forward and see backward and see all around us at the same time. Our histories are who we are.

I'd like to make two final points. The first one is that, when I was a student in university, I realized that there was a dilemma for the white American writer. The first real dilemma that he or she faces, is that they are displaced. When you leave the bones of your ancestors, you become a wanderer. Unfortunately, the message of the wanderer is one that isn't always healthy. So, American literature has not truly reflected the "angst" that exists in American culture. How do we make our literature as important as they seem to think their literature is?

The second thing I'd like to mention is that for many of our people, we're the first generation to be in print. We are few in numbers and it's important that we lay a groundwork for our children and the young writers that are here. We can't do that unless we become activists for our children and for our people. I would like to see a whole table of petitions, and see you take the petitions wherever you go and have people sign them. Our place in world literature is a small place. Thank you.

Kelly Morgan (*Lakota*)

It is my contention that the study of American Indian literature should be separate from the study of American literature. As a canon in and of itself, American Indian literature is separate from American literature because it is, one, written specifically by American Indians, and two, is about American Indian people and their cultures. The bulk of material that represents the oral and written history of American Indian literature is large enough that it warrants the separation of the American canon from the American Indian canon, specifically in order for the student of American Indian literature to sort out the complexity of the materials, both criticism of American literature and American Indian literature itself.

The separation of these two literatures is warranted by the continuing problem of the presence of frauds, like Jamake Highwater and Lynn C. Andrews. Ironically, the separation of the two literatures would validate their works as American literature, because they are certainly not American Indian in origin, and it would create a space for such "wannabe" Indians. It would make clear to the student of American Indian literature those works which are written by non-Indian scholars of American Indian literature and cultures.

I see it necessary to organize American Indian literature according to two approaches, traditional and contemporary. The teaching of American Indian literature should include basic courses in oral literature, written literature, poetry, etc.; literatures being taught in accordance with the two approaches mentioned. It should include core courses in major and minor authors, from which class instruction is geared toward illuminating the cultural world view each author focuses on in their work. The thing to remember is that American Indian literature is changing, just as any other literature changes with the changing of the cultures and societies they describe.

By traditional American Indian writing, I mean traditional literature which is produced by and for American Indians, which is intended for American Indian use with no impulse to write for non-Indians. It is essential to separate the courses on American Indian literatures.

It is my perspective that you cannot learn the truth about America and American history unless you look at American Indian literature and how American Indian cultures have been affected. At the same time, it is a known fact that we, as First Americans with cultures which functioned primarily and foremost in contrast to mainstream American culture, don't want to have anything to do with being associated within the same world view as that of other Americans.

Finally, American literature, and American literature about American Indians, is quite dissimilar from American Indian literatures. American Indian literatures have a complex and culturally diverse background, as well as a clear future in the publishing world. Thank you.

Daniel David Moses (*Delaware*)

When I hear the world literature label, I think that this is something that should be taught in universities, something that is part of the broad world and should represent humanity at large, and I get to another side of the image of what canon means, like there's something perfect and ideal. I start getting real suspicious about that and wonder if that is how we're supposed to be measuring what's good in our writing. I wonder what's good in the way that people think about the best that the human race can do.

In Canada, there was a conference of First Nations writers at a town called Duck Lake in Saskatchewan. At one point, I noticed one of my friends was talking with this lady and she was showing him a sheaf of papers. There was his name in there with a number of the stuff he'd written. She was putting together a curriculum of Native Studies and I thought, "I wonder if there's anything of mine in there?" She was using one of my poems and I was glad she was using it but I was kind of jealous that my friend was getting more of his writings in it than I was.

I guess she was sensitive, or maybe feeling guilty about it, because I was standing right there in front of her, and she said, "Well I did read your other play, but I felt it was too controversial for our students." I was kind of flabbergasted because I thought I had just written the truth. In fact, I think just because I was looking for a certain kind of aesthetic in the play when I was writing it, that I had actually taken some of the real rawness of the situation out it and tried to put some beauty in it to sugarcoat the bitterness in it. I never thought it was controversial. I thought it would be accepted fact.

So that's part of what the canon is about. There's some medicine that non-Natives don't want to swallow. There are reasons for medicine. I think there's a big sickness in world literature that some of our writings can assuage, if not necessarily cure. At the same time, non-Native people have got to do a lot of the work themselves. They're always looking to us for answers, but part of it is just paying attention to your own belly button.

These are just some of the traps that I see if we go and measure ourselves by non-Native standards. I think we've always got to remember that there is a human heart at the center of any world-class literature. In that big culture out there, that's not something the dominant culture is always looking for. Sometimes they're looking for things that are just the latest trends. I think we've always got to remind ourselves where we're coming from, and what we've been taught are important matters, and not allow ourselves to be distracted. Some of the fireworks that go on in world literature are just amazing! If we can keep part of ourselves always at home, I think we can avoid a lot of the traps. That's all I have to say.

Jeannette C. Armstrong (*Okanagan*)

There is indeed a canon of literature that is there, that has always been there, and will continue to be there. It is central and integral to our survival as a people. It is central and integral in terms of our resistance to the continuing onslaught of colonization, which erodes our communities and damages our people.

Using our literatures to reestablish health, not only in our communities, but to establish health in those sick communities out there that are destroying not only our world, but almost the entire world around us is important. We see our literatures, our voice, as a mechanism of healing ourselves, as medicine to the societies, bringing the possibility of a better future, a more healthy future, not only for our children, but also the children of other peoples in the world.

We are instruments. We, as thinking beings, are instruments of transformation. We are the transformers of societies. We, as Native peoples, can transform this world. We can transform the sickness in this world through the power of our words, through the power of our stories, through the power that comes from the basis of our societies. Societies founded in the spiritual values that are contained in the principles of cooperation that our people consistently display in our communities here in North America, and other indigenous communities world over have an interconnectedness with all of the environment. Unfortunately, we are not teaching our children how much transforming we have done in terms of changing the thinking of the human beings, and the kind of treatment that Europeans consistently lived with and promoted before coming into contact with people who are truly democratic.

I think it is extremely important that we continue to reinforce for ourselves—to each other and with each other—those thoughts and feelings when we're alone back home. It's very difficult to survive. Sometimes it's very difficult to continue the work. Sometimes, it's so overwhelming and easy to say, we can't make it, it's not possible. But we can transform this society as a unit, as a group, together, in solidarity.

We are medicine. We are the healers. And we are sacred, every one of us. Every one of us has been given a sacred life, we've been given the gift of life, and we've been empowered by that gift of life with the ability to think, with memory, and with the ability to transform our thinking into action. In that sense, each one of us is very, very powerful, and that's a very sacred responsibility that we have. It seems that our literature is about responsibility to our people, to our survival, to our Creator. Thank you.

SESSION FOUR
EARTH AND THE CIRCLE OF LIFE

Native Writers and the Environment

Eleanor Sioui (*Huron/Wyandot*)

I would like to speak about the earth, Mother Earth, and the way American Indian ecology could help cure our sick mother. It's our ecological way to bring all the learned people of the world to try and cure the world, to try and cure all the new sicknesses popping up they cannot understand. They cannot cure them because, I believe, those sicknesses, those maladies, are coming from our sick mother, and as long as the Mother Earth can't be cured, we're going to be a disappearing people on this planet, and all that is living on this planet will also disappear.

All things/beings are connected. All things/beings have a soul: the moon, the sun, the air, the earth, plants, trees, rivers, mountains. We have all the power and duty to cure the soul of Mother Earth. She is dying now of an old malady and it's our duty to revive the concepts of love and respect for all living creatures of the cosmos. We must redirect the creative power of the mind, heart, and soul. We are becoming too technical and not spiritual enough.

The sap which courses through the trees carries the memory of the red man. Now, the trail of tears of the red man has become trails of contamination in our mother world. Garden spirits walk with us on our journey to revive the planet. May our voices find resonance in the field of a new world of literature. That literature, I think, should be written by all of American Indian descent who come from all the countries of North and South America. Be they black American Indians, Latin American Indians, or whatever, we all have the same roots.

The time has arrived to embrace Mother Earth with the sweetness and strength of the voices of our people in their writing. From all the four corners of America's continent, south, north, west, east, speaking all languages, Indian, English, French, Spanish, Portuguese, etcetera, we must bring to our Mother Earth our souls, minds, bodies, and hearts to fill up the emptiness left by our carelessness. We must wrap Mother Earth in the melodies of the cries and laughter of our babies, children, youth, elders, and give our Mother Earth a refreshing breath of life. This is the ecological, creative curing power of American Indian poets, and I thank you.

Linda Hogan (*Chickasaw*)

We had a pact, an agreement, a sacred trust with the land that was thousands of years old, before European presence on this continent. We had complex systems of agriculture and tradition and religion, and knowledge about what is now called ecology.

We're all wounded, not just Indian people, but all of us have been wounded by the culture that has split us from the natural world, from our inner lives, and from our dreams. When we were broken as people, so was the bond between us and the land, the sacred agreement that we had. In not many years after colonization, after what is sometimes called exploration, but what we call conquest, the environment was already severely affected. So what is happening to the environment isn't just happening now, it's been happening all along.

In 1978, the Religious Freedoms Act was passed. Most non-Indian people don't realize that in 1894, all Indian religions were banned by the Bureau of Indian Affairs in the United States. So it was illegal for us to practice our own traditions until 1978, and there were people incarcerated for practicing traditional religions. The Freedom of Religion Act really focuses a great deal on land issues, on sacred sites, on the destruction of sacred sites. We're the only people whose religion has ties to the land in this country.

Sacred is an interesting word to think about what the meaning of it is. I heard someone once define sacred as that which could be destroyed but could not be created. I think it's important to look at that when we're thinking about what has happened to the land and the treaties that have been broken that had to do with land and a different concept of ownership. Being owned by the land is how Native people see it, rather than owning it which means being able to build boundaries and walls and fences that separates and parcels out the land.

Barney Bush (*Shawnee*)

A great deal of time throughout history has been spent warring over the concepts of truth and fiction, science and religion, black and white, the Native world and the Colonial world. If any history written by the hands of conquerors is accurate, it is then safe to say that the thousands of years prior to the coming of Europeans to these eastern Turtle Island shores are quite simply not a part of the invaders' history. The years prior to the coming of the white man here is not part of their history. The accomplishments made in this country and the respect for nature and the land and the earth has nothing to do with 1492.

The cultural evolutions were accomplished independently, for better or worse, in sickness and health, and until death did us part. When the Europeans decided to name their conquest America, they became the first Americans. Native peoples in our homelands were the first American casualties, and it is safer for the first Americans to teach their history in our country as if it were a sack of eggs.

Why do you think Native history in this country has been taught to us so poorly? Because it is written by the colonizer. How can they tell the truth? It would mean they would have to change their way of life. Greed would have to be surrendered. The entire dissipation of the balance of life, earth nature, human nature and spiritual nature, is upon us as we confer about minor obstacles of nouns and pronouns, Democrats and Republicans, and the oppression that happens in other countries, but not in America.

I'm not going through the list of what people have done to this planet, and what the greed of mankind is doing, and why people are coming to Indians for answers. They don't need to come to us for answers. They don't need to hang around the corners and see what's going on. They know the difference between right and wrong. They don't need to be coming out and standing at Indian ceremonies. They don't need to be there. They've got their own ceremonies. They need to teach them to their people to see if it will make them act respectful to the land and to the people, and if it doesn't, they're doing the wrong thing. They need to understand that when you strip mine the earth, when you tear up the land, you have destroyed the natural shape of the land for eternity, or eternity as long as we know it. You've upset the whole balance of things for the eternity of the area.

Finally, I say to the brothers and sisters who are in Central America and South America, that you're in for a long, hard row of stumps to hoe. That colonization in that part of the country is as absurd and as dangerous and as two-faced as any colonial kind of mess on the face of this earth. People who do not choose to die or suffer, are dying and suffering, right down to the little kids, to the old people. And so is the earth. You can't have one without the other. I do not apologize for sounding tough, because that's the way I feel.

Elizabeth Woody (*Warm Springs/Yakima/ Wasco/Navajo*)

My grandparents taught me, and my uncles and aunties, that to love the land was a good thing to do. But what we have been doing lately is fighting on behalf of the land, on behalf of the animals, and I think what people tend to forget is that the earth is a changing thing, the animals are a changing thing. So, the story I hear is how the earth's patterns are shifting.

I'm going to tell you a story to illustrate my feelings about the land. I again think about the music I hear. I hear songs in my dreams, which is unusual since I do not know any songs, or even know Indian. I think of it as this. The music comes from the tapping of our finger, beating out the occasional soft song, the way a river sounds while we fish, and the sound of the life, dragonflies flying, singing to me. The music mingles and makes these songs that sound through my dreams. Maybe I catch the hum of the mountain over there too. He's waiting you see, to get involved with that fiery young woman he sees at the corner of his eyes. Mountain love is a real, shaky, fired-up affair. They push up great hilly ranges, bend over the lakes, rub up against one another so willingly, that it takes years to cover up all that passion, that rumbling and love-talk. Once my grandmother said that her great-grandmother and aunt had to run their horses into a lake, to cover themselves with wet hides, to keep from getting burned. The water was so hot it took all their courage to stay put. I believe this was the last rumble before the mountains curled up for a good sleep. When I told one of my science teachers about this, he said that these stories are just myths, not fact, and that mountains don't even erupt around here anymore. I believed him. Until Mt. St. Helens erupted. It erased all innocent belief in the fabled absolutes in science, for me. Thank goodness, I had heard some facts about those mountains way before I entered school.

Lincoln Tritt (*Gwichin Athabascan*)

Usually, when you hear of wisdom it's attributed to elders because wisdom is gained by constant exposure or constant experience with certain things all your life. That's one of the biggest differences between the Native people and today's people. Native people, for the most part, believe in things that they don't see. That builds up your faith and your spiritual belief is a lot stronger when you're not always out there looking for proof. Today, you always have to produce some kind of paper to say that what you say is right, or to say that you're honest, or whatever. I wouldn't think much of myself if I had to have a paper to prove that I'm honest.

We've all been out in the woods, I'm sure. When you go out into the woods you look around you and you learn. You know what the season is like. The difficulty of living in that harsh environment is that it forces the people to work together, and when you work together, you have to have certain things within the society.

One thing within that society is that you can't have anybody with more power than anybody else. That would make them stick out among the people. Everything our people did, they did together. So, everybody has to be of equal value, importance. Having people all equal is very important to the idea of unity.

The other thing you have to have in Native society is not thinking in terms of me. Ego is very damaging to the concept of unity. Our elders, when they speak, even when they're talking about themselves, they sound like they're referring to somebody else, because they don't direct anything toward themselves. When they make decisions, they think in terms of the tribe first, and then they think about themselves, because you are not a member of the tribe, you are the tribe. What you do reflects on the tribe. If I do something embarrassing, the tribe would be embarrassed. If I do something good, the tribe would be proud. So, you have to think in terms of the group.

Everything around you is given to you by the Great Spirit. Life is given to you by the Great Spirit, so you appreciate life, you appreciate everything you get. These things end up in the people being very humble, spiritually strong, respectful, and very appreciative of life. This is how our people had their system set up. If you look at the original, the pre-contact Native system, you'll find everything in there. You'll find an education system as well as a structured social system. Everything you learn about today's society is in there too, but it's from a very different perspective.

IN THE CLASSROOM

COMBINING VOICE WITH VISION

James Bruchac (*Abenaki*)

Having grown up the son of Abenaki writer, editor, and storyteller Joseph Bruchac, I, unlike many others of my generation, was fully aware that Native American literature did indeed exist. It was a strange night when my brother Jesse and I did not go to sleep to the sound of a typewriter echoing from my father's study. Even to this day, two decades later, when I hear the snapping sound of a typewriter's keys, a sound now replaced by the soft thumps of a computer keyboard, it brings back memories of my childhood, memories that include the many legends my father would share with us on those long winter nights, told to us even before the nightly typewriter tradition.

Still, as with most Native writers of that time, despite the fact that my father's typewriter would never go cold, it would be years before any of those legends, poems, novels, or stories would make it into books and even longer before they would make it into classrooms. It wasn't until 1987, my second year of college, that I was able to refer to Native-authored writings in one of my literature classes. It was in that class, focusing on American folklore, that I wrote an essay comparing traditional Native American legends (including, not by chance, several familiar stories my father had recorded) with a collection of pioneer folklore. In the essay I pointed out various cultural and spiritual differences concerning the land, animals, and the natural world in general, as well as discussing how such Native legends effected my perceptions, not unlike several lesson plans in this section. Unfortunately, my teacher was not aware of such Native literature or expression. Despite the fact that I received a passing grade, the lack of support in the academic community kept such writings out of most classrooms.

Now, less than ten years later, the amount of Native literature published and available to the general public has increased drastically. In 1995, seeing a Native authored book in the front window of your local bookstore has become quite prevalent. Witnessing this increase first hand, within our own family business, The North American Native Authors Distribution Catalog (specializing in the promotion and sale of Native authored books), has been a great experience. Since 1987, we have added hundreds of new titles, by numerous publishers, written principally by first-time authors. An increase in Native literature resulted in the growth of the catalog from eight to fifty-two pages. Along with this growth, we have experienced an increase in the number of schools—both Native and non-Native—ordering from the catalog. Unlike my primary and secondary school years, the use of Native American literature in contemporary classrooms has become quite common. Traditional legends, poetry, fiction, and autobiographical writings are providing greater understanding and interest in the study of both the past and contemporary Native experience.

For Native students, after hundreds of years reading books written by predominately non-Native authors from a non-Native point of view, the use of Native authored literature has been nothing short of an educational revolution. Literature such as those suggested in the following lesson plans by Native authors and editors such as Simon Ortiz, Joy Harjo, Lance Henson, Gladys Cardiff, and Linda Hogan as well as many others offer to the Native students familiar voices and experiences. These voices and experiences, in my view, can serve to inspire Native students to read and, hopefully, to write as well.

This initial inspiration, however, as with my past experience writing about my own insights and experiences, does not always mean the full understanding and encouragement of a teacher. This can happen especially if that teacher is non-Native and/or has no understanding of Native expression or experience. It was to address such obstacles that resulted in holding classroom workshops following the 1992 Returning The Gift Festival.

The outreach program's workshops, involved Native writers going into schools throughout Indian Country. They provided a very personal introduction and interpretation of Native literature and, more important, and overall inspiration for writing. Students involved in these classroom workshops were able to have person-to-person learning relationships with such Native authors as Rudy Martin (*Tewa/Navajo/Apache*), Lance Henson (*Cheyenne*), Joseph Bruchac (*Abenaki*), Gladys Cardiff (*Cherokee*), Cochise Anderson (*Chickasaw/Choctaw*), Roberta Hill Whiteman (*Wisconsin Oneida*), and Jeanetta Calhoun (*Delaware/Lenni Lenape*).

Reflecting back on these workshops, it may seem hard to compare any other form of curriculum with such a personable approach. However, the resulting Lesson Plans from these workshops can serve as a valuable tool for Native and non-Natives alike. With the Lesson Plans in this section, teachers can help students draw on the ideas found in the Native literature and to write about their own life experiences and influences.

In the following Lesson Plans, several important sources of inspiration are stressed, such as drawing on an individual's traditional legends, spirituality, and sense of place. There are also other sources of inspiration such as in Lesson Plan #7, developed by Roberta Hill Whiteman, in which students are asked to write about their most precious memories; Lesson Plan #8, developed by Jeanetta Calhoun, in which students write about the importance of their family heritage.

All of the Lesson Plans and writing exercises are aimed at the importance of drawing on who an individual is as a person and finding their own voice. Taking on ideas related to personal identity and expression is an excellent approach to use with students of all cultures and traditions. Additional inspiration which came out of the original writing workshops can be found in the final section, ANTHOLOGY OF EMERGING NATIVE VOICES which is a sample of the work of students both in and out of the classroom.

Hopefully, as we continue to build on the many outcomes of the original Returning The Gift Festival, including the classroom information found in this anthology, as well as projects like Wordcraft Circle, the future for Native literature will become even brighter. And although Native literature appears to be in a time of positive transition, a "Renaissance" as some may prefer, it can only continue if each generation is provided with the appropriate inspiration to write. It is the inspiration from generation to generation which is constantly combining voice with vision.

THE OUTREACH PROGRAM: WRITER'S WORKSHOPS

Lesson Plan: #1

Developed by: Rudy Martin (*Tewa/Navajo/Apache*)
Grade Level: K-12
Texts: See Appendix 1.
            "Deer Hunter and White Corn Maiden," *American Indian Myths and Legends*, Richard Erdoes and Alfonso Ortiz. Pantheon Fairy Tale & Folklore Library, 1984.

            "Vision Bundle," "O Honeysuckle Woman," and "I Have Not Signed A Treaty with the U. S. Government," *Not Vanishing: A collection of Poems*. chrystos. Press Gang Publishers, 1988.

Discussion:

As an introduction, I used a translation by Alfonso Ortiz of a Tewa story, "Deer Hunter and White Corn Maiden." This was part of a collection called *American Indian Myths and Legends* by Richard Erdoes and Alfonso Ortiz, published by Pantheon Fairy Tale & Folklore Library in 1984.

I wanted to show how translations of traditional Native stories can be properly interpreted. Properly in the sense that it is more than language. It is inflection. Something that cannot be duplicated by a non-Indian.

I also hoped to display how the roots of Native American literature are in our oral histories and traditional stories.

I used three poems by chrystos, "Vision Bundle," "O Honeysuckle Woman," and "I Have Not Signed a Treaty with the U. S. Government." All three poems are from her *Not Vanishing* collection published in 1988 by Press Gang publishers.

The poem, "Vision Bundle" I reinforced by including two articles

I've written about Native Spirituality and the exploitation issues surrounding the subject. The articles are "Medicine War" published by the Ute Bulletin and "Medicine War II - Bad Medicine" published in *The Lakota Times* (now *Indian Country Today*).

"*O Honeysuckle Woman*" allowed for discussion regarding Native people's relationship to the environment. The clan systems and how we are able to communicate with plants and animals was also part of the discussion. I wanted to show how this relationship is traditionally used in our literature.

"I Have Not Signed A Treaty with the U. S. Government" was an opportunity to understand the anger and bitterness that many Native people have in terms of our history.

Writing Exercises:

1. Write a poem focused on personal experiences with spirituality/religion
2. Write a poem describing yourself or someone you know as a plant or animal
3. Write a poem about your personal political observations.

Lesson Plan #2

Developed by: Lance Henson (*Cheyenne*)
Grade Level: K-12
Texts: See Appendix 2.
          "We Are The People." Traditional Lakota Sioux song sung by Red Bird, 19th century.

          Warrior Nation Trilogy. Lance Henson
          from *A Cheyenne Sketchbook*, The Greenfield Review Press, 1992

Discussion:

Red Bird was a Lakota Sioux who lived in the 19th century. The Lakota Sioux people have long been friends and allies of the Cheyenne and their way of life is very similar. Red Bird's song is the opening prayer for the Sun Dance, a very important ceremony still practiced by both the

Cheyenne and the Lakota Sioux nations. During the Sun Dance, young men go without food and drink for several days and dance facing the sun. This is done as a prayer to ask the Creator to help all of the people. Although Red Bird's song is very short and seems simple, it has powerful meaning.

Lance Henson is a contemporary Cheyenne Indian poet from the southern plains. Praise for the natural works is a very important part of Native American life. Such praise is evident in Lance Henson's poem. The natural world is very much a part of this Native writer's life, not something which is outside or separated from him. It is as close to him as his family.

It can be pointed out that both Red Bird's song and Lance Henson's poem are written in very clear simple language. The language is direct. Even though there are mysterious things here—things such as being able to "send a voice," "breathe with the rivers" and hear "the song of the stones," it seems as if both the song and the poem are meant to communicate and not confuse.

As part of the discussion, talk about the way in which the Native people of the Great Plains were "buffalo people," relying on the buffalo for their food and clothing, their fuel and tools, using every part of each animal they killed for which they gave thanks to it's spirit. Even though they hunted the buffalo, they respected it and thought of it as their brother.

Discussion Questions:

1. Who do the students think "Grandfather" is in Red Bird's song?
2. What does it mean when Red Bird says "I will live?" (*NOTE: When Red Bird says, "I will live" in his song, he is asking for help. He means that "with the help and blessing of the Creator, I will be able to survive." The "Grandfather," he speaks to in this song is Wakan Tanka, the Great Spirit.*)
3. In American Indian life, the earth is thought of as our mother who takes care of us and gives us life. How is this like or unlike the usual American way of viewing the earth or the animals?
4. What things does the poet Lance Henson seem to like about the natural world.?
5. How is the natural world connected to Lance Henson?
6. How do you explain such mysterious statements as:
   a. we are the buffalo people?
   b. we alone hear the song of the stones?

7. What do you think it means to "send a voice" in Red Bird's song?

8. Why is this song so short? (*NOTE: One traditional Native American singer once said, "Our songs are so short because our people know so much.*) Can you compare the shortness of these songs with the short poems of another culture such as the haiku poems of the people of Japan?

9. How is the end of Red Bird's song different from its beginning? What happens in this song-poem?

10. How is Lance Henson's poem similar to Red Bird's traditional song? (*NOTE: Simple direct language; the mysterious quality of the poem; the way the singer of this song-poem views the natural world as one views a family; the way both use repetition.*)

Writing Exercises:

1. Write a class poem on a "We Are The People who . . ." theme, using clear language and a structure like that of Lance Henson's poem to describe "our own" lives.

2. Write an individual poem in which you imagine yourself as one of the buffalo people. Describe what your life is like, bearing in mind such things as being thankful and positive, and viewing the earth as a part of your life.

3. Write a poem in which you ask for help from others. Keep the language simple and direct. Make references to the natural world and use repetitive structure.

Lesson Plan #3

Developed by: Joseph Bruchac III (*Abenaki*)

Grade Level: 11th

Texts: See Appendix 3.

        "Formula for Obtaining Long Life" from the manuscript of Swimmer, a 19th century Cherokee doctor.

        "Long Person." Gladys Cardiff.

Discussion:

The Cherokee people originally lived in the southern part of what is now the United States in the area of the states of Georgia and North Carolina. They quickly adopted many of the ways of their white neighbors and by the early 1800's were living in houses like their white friends and wearing European style clothing because they had decided the best way to survive was to be like the whites. Because of this, they and the Seminole, Choctaw, Chickasaw, and Creek people were called "The Five Civilized Tribes." They maintained their own language and customs. When a brilliant Cherokee man named Sequoiah developed, in the early 1800's, a syllabic alphabet in which to write the Cherokee language, the rest of the Cherokee people were quick to learn it. In less than 10 years, more than 90% of the Cherokee people could read and write in their new written language and there were newspapers and books being published in Cherokee. Sadly, however, gold was discovered on their southern lands and the greed of white people—with the help of the U. S. government—drove the Cherokee from their lands. They were forced, during the time Andrew Jackson was President of the United States, to travel west to what is now Oklahoma. Many died on their long journey. Today, Cherokee people live all over the United States with many still in North Carolina and Oklahoma.

Swimmer was a late 19th century Cherokee traditional doctor. His poem was originally written using the Cherokee syllabic script in a notebook he kept. It is a formula, like a doctor's prescription. By going to the river at dawn and speaking this beautiful poem, it is believed a person may obtain a longer life.

Gladys Cardiff is a contemporary Cherokee poet. Although she lives in the Pacific Northwest, much of her work refers to Cherokee traditions and to places which remain sacred to the Cherokee people.

The language in both of these writings is very direct. Both poems, like most Native American poetry, are strongly connected to nature. However, there are things in both poems which may be hard for someone who knows little about Cherokee traditional culture to understand.

Discussion questions:
1. Both Swimmer's traditional formula and Gladys Cardiff's poem refer to the "Long Person." Who or what is this? Have the students discuss this and see if they can figure it out from the context. (*NOTE: "Long Person" is the respectful term used by the Cherokee to refer to a river.*)

2. What other words/phrases are hard to understand? Make a list of these things and then discuss them seeing if you can understand them better when you know the meaning of "Long Person." (*NOTE: Other Cherokee traditional beliefs include the belief that white is a good color which is connected with spiritual purity and that seven is a very magical number. Descriptions in Cherokee stories are often in sevens: seven hills, seven brothers, and so on.*)

3. What words or phrases in the Swimmer formula refer to the "Long Person?" Are they easier to understand when you know what the "Long Person" is?

4. How does Gladys Cardiff bring in the natural world in her poem? What similes does she use?

5. What is Oconoluftee? What does the use of this word add to the poem?

6. What is the structure of Gladys Cardiff's poem? (*NOTE: Part of its structure is that it begins with a description of an old photo and ends with language which is much like that of the Cherokee formula of Swimmer.*)

7. Who is Gladys Cardiff describing and how do we see that person. (*NOTE: It is her grandfather in a photograph which shows the old man in front of his blacksmith shop with her own father and uncle.*)

8. In what way is her poem similar to or different from Swimmer's formula?

9. What is the purpose of the Swimmer formula? Does Gladys Cardiff's poem have a similar purpose or a different one? Do poems have to have a purpose?

Writing Exercises:

1. Imagine yourself going to a river or a feature of nature such as a mountain or lake that is very powerful. What would you say to that natural feature in a poem? Think of what you would call it (in the way the Cherokee call a river "Long Person.") What kind of help might it be able to give you? Now write a poem in which you address that natural feature.

2. Look at an old photograph of your own grandfather or grandmother and write a poem in which you describe what you see. Also being in something of their own traditional heritage. Every-

one has a traditional heritage. It may be European, African, Asian, or even American Indian. You may want to include a word or two in the language spoken by your ancestors if English was not their mother tongue. Structure your poem like Gladys Cardiff's poem and make use of natural similes.

Lesson Plan #4

Developed by: M. Cochise Anderson (*Chickasaw/Choctaw*)
Grade Level: K-12
Texts: See Appendix 4.
        "From My Grandmother," *Dancing On The Rim of the World*. Jo Whitehorse Cochran (Lakota). Sun Tracks and the University of Arizona Press, Tucson. 1990.

        "Old Ones Who Whisper," *Nitassin/Norte Terre*. M. Cochise Anderson (Chickasaw/Choctaw). Special 20/21 (issue). 1990.

Discussion:
    Continuance is a recurring theme in Native American thought and is addressed throughout much of Native poetry. Symbolized by the "Sacred Hoop" or "Circle of Life," this entails respect for those who came before us (elders) and those who will follow our path (the youth). The circle is all inclusive, ever expansive, and tolerant of all life. Seathe (Chief Seattle) said, "We are all connected." (i.e., ancestor, man, brother, mother, sister, elder, child, animal, tree, rock, water, etc..) The concept of give and take is inherent in the circle way of life. Recognizing our own mortality and yet acknowledging our enduring spirit, a strength in that spirit is passed on to the next generation.
    In Jo Whitehorse Cochran's poem, "From My Grandmother," many of these ideas are readily apparent. This conversation is a remembrance and a recognition of self
    In M. Cochise Anderson's poem, "Old Ones Who Whisper," continuance is also a pervading idea. The poem's voice moves from one of remembrance to one of belief. (Even though the belief is in something intangible.)

Discussion Questions:

1. In the poem "From My Grandmother," who are the Old Ones? What are vision/dreams and what do they mean in this poem?
2. What does M. Cochise Anderson mean by "So I know who watches over/(But) it's a secret to me." in his poem, "Old Ones Who Whisper?" How does the author recognize his mortality? How does that convey continuance?
3. How do the authors of both poems bring past and present together?
4. What do the authors feel in their remembrances and projections?

Writing Exercises:

1. Write a poem talking as one of the Old Ones (tree, river, grandparent, neighborhood . . .) or speaking to an Old One.
2. A tradition or custom also speaks to a continuing heritage or lineage. Write a poem about a custom or tradition which you would like to pass on to your children.

Lesson Plan #5

Developed by: M. Cochise Anderson (*Chickasaw/Choctaw*)
Grade Level: K-12
Texts: See Appendix 5.
          "Telling About Coyote," *Shaking The Pumpkin: Traditional Poetry of the Indian North American*. Simon Ortiz (Acoma Pueblo). University of New Mexico Press, Albuquerque. 1986.

          "Broken Tradition," *Dancing On The Rim Of The World*. Vince Wannassay (Umatilla). Sun Tracks and The University of Arizona Press, Tucson. 1990.

Discussion:

Animals and animal spirits have played an important part in Native people's way of thinking and living. Animals were yet another connection to ourselves. Many young people ask, "How did Native people know which berries and nuts were poisonous?" The answer, of course, is that they watched the animals and saw what foods they ate and what foods they didn't eat.

Another custom among Native people was that when an animal was slain, they thanked the animal spirit for allowing it to help sustain the people's life (meat for food, hides for clothing and shelter, and bones for utensils such as sewing needles).

The relationship with the animal world was very revered by Native people. Many stories about how the animals helped Native people pervades throughout the many Nations here on Turtle Island. Sometimes they helped the people by showing what not to do. One such animal character is Old Man Coyote. Coyote is somewhat of a messenger for the Creator who can take many forms. Coyote can be male or female. Coyote can be wise or foolish or even be another animal or person. Whatever the form, Coyote's role is to show the people their faults and virtues, and in that manner help them live the proper way.

In Simon Ortiz's poem, "Telling About Coyote," Old Coyote is seen as a schemer and selfish character. However, the author never condemns Old Coyote. He even has a certain sentiment for Coyote which has some humorous side effects.

In Vince Wannassay's poem, "Broken Tradition," a dead squirrel is his metaphor for broken traditions. Again, the animal is a helper in reminding the author of his own identity; the squirrel re-affirms it.

Discussion Questions:

1. How is Coyote seen in the poem, "Telling About Coyote"? Why? Is Coyote a positive or a negative influence?
2. What do the descriptions of Coyote's fur and Crow's feathers mean in the poem?
3. What does the passage, "He'll be back./Don't worry./He'll be back." allude to?
4. What does the dead squirrel represent in the poem "Broken Tradition"?
5. What tradition is it that the author says Squirrel should have stuck to?
6. What other metaphors does the author of "Broken Tradition" use to make his point?

Writing Exercises:

1. Write a poem about an animal or animal character whose behavior reflects your own. (The animal could be a dog, a cat, a bird, etc. . . .)
2. Write a poem describing the relationship between animals and humans from a specific animal's point of view.

Lesson Plan #6

Developed by: Roberta Hill Whiteman (*Wisconsin Oneida*)
Grade Level: 3rd
Texts: Poems translated from the Quechua by Mark Strand.

Discussion:

Because students often need a clear task rather than a suggestion, I used materials with which I was familiar. I recited a few poems, among them "Dirty Dinky" by Theodore Roethke, and some poems translated from the Quechua by Mark Strand.

Discussion Questions:

1. How does the sound of the rain sound like Ah?
2. How does a person, going from door to door, seem like a feather?
3. The Quechua poem uses the sound and movement of the rain cloud. What other feelings might a person have if they were born in a rain cloud? (*NOTE: sometimes students will consider the moisture [wet], or the silence, or the lightning.*)

Writing Exercises:

I read a poem from the *COMPAS Anthology* called "The Brazil Nut With Nine Faces." Than I have the students choose a nut (brazil, almond, or hazelnut). Their task is to explore the nut with their senses and make comparisons. The students write down their comparisons.

I then ask the students to think about how the nut might also be exploring them. I ask them to write down what the nut would say to them.

Lesson Plan # 7

Developed by: Roberta Hill Whiteman (*Wisconsin Oneida*)
Grade Level: 4th-8th
Texts: See Appendix 6.
          "Remember." Joy Harjo (Muscogee)

Discussion:

The objective of this lesson is to tap into their own memories and capture it in slow motion. The poem by Joy Harjo was used as a model.

Discussion Questions:

1. Who do you think the poet is talking to? (*NOTE: The poem has the familiarity of an older person addressing a younger person.*)
2. Are there any unusual persons in this poem? Who are they? (*NOTE: students usually point out the wind and the moon and this is an opportunity to point out how in Native cultures the universe is alive.*)
3. List some of your memories such as your "first kiss," the first day of school, the first bike crash, rides at the fair, waking up on a spring morning, baseball games, etc..
4. Take a memory and cluster images around it. What do you see, hear, taste, touch, smell at that time?

Lesson Plan #8

Developed by: Jeanetta Calhoun (*Delaware/Lenni Lenape*)
Grade Level: K-12
Texts: See Appendix 7.
          "Heritage." Linda Hogan (*Chickasaw*)

Discussion:

Linda Hogan is a member of the Chickasaw Nation. She was born in

Denver and grew up in Oklahoma. She is a poet, novelist, and is also licensed to care for injured wild animals in her home.

Discussion Questions:

1. Discuss what "heritage" means. Does it mean the same thing to the students as it does to Linda Hogan?
2. Discuss the usage of the word "brown." Does it color the poem or suggest an emotion?
3. How does Linda Hogan feel about her family and her upbringing? Is there a reason that she talks about her grandmother more than she does about the rest of her family?
4. What is the writer's heritage?
5. What does the writer mean when she says "my whiteness a shame"? (*NOTE: She had the lightest complexion of everyone in her father's family. It is difficult for many mixed-blood Native people to "fit in," either in the Native world or the world of the non-Native.*)
6. Why was the writer's father told not to remember the songs? (*NOTE: During the mid-1900s, Native languages and life-ways were not only unacceptable, but in many instances, illegal.*)

Writing Exercises:

1. Write a poem about your personal family heritage. Describe your parents and grandparents and what they have given you. This should include not only physical heirlooms, but also emotional re-membrances.
2. Choose a color which you feel describes your life right now. Write a poem in which that color is a central image used in different contexts. (See the fifth stanza of "Heritage" for an example.)

BEYOND THE CLASSROOM

THE WORDCRAFT CIRCLE VISION

Lee Francis (*Laguna Pueblo*)

The evening of the first day of the Festival an Awards Banquet was scheduled. After dinner, the presentation of awards began. There were the First Book Awards: The Diane Decorah Memorial Award for Poetry presented to Joe Dale Tate Nevaquaya (*Comanche/Yuchi*) for *Leaving Holes*, and to Gloria Bird (*Spokane*) for *Moon Over The Reservation*. The Louis Littlecoon Oliver Memorial Award for Short Fiction was presented to Robert Perea (*Oglala Lakota*) for *Stacy's Story*. The Richard Margolis Memorial Award for Creative Non-Fiction was presented to Melissa Fawcett Sayet (*Mohegan*) for *The Lasting of the Mohicans*, and the Drama Award went to William S. Yellow Robe, Jr. (*Assiniboine*) for his play, *The Star Quilter*. N. Scott Momaday, the Pulitzer prize winner for literature, was the recipient of the Lifetime Achievement Award. I remember thinking that the only award missing was one for the best student writer.

On the second day of the Festival, I approached organizers Joseph Bruchac III, Geary Hobson, and Rayna Green. "What" I asked, "did I need to do so that an award could be presented to the best Native student writer?" It was suggested that I meet with the students as well as established writers and talk it over with them. The following day, we met to talk about presenting an award to the best Native student writer.

Among those participating in that meeting were established, published Native writers and storytellers Barney Bush (*Shawnee/Cayuga*) and Bruce King (*Oneida*) as well as beginning and emerging Native student writers which included Penny Olson (*Sault Ste. Marie Chippewa*), Eddie Webb (*Tsalagi*), Hershman John (*Navajo*), Anne Begay (*Navajo*), and her daughter Kathy Peltier (*Navajo/Sioux*). As we visited about giving an award to the best Native student writer, the students were politely silent. I explained that I felt it was important to celebrate the accomplishments of young Native writers. Presenting a student award would, in my view, emphasize the importance of the writings by beginning and emerging Native writers and storytellers.

Eddie Webb spoke up and said that he understood what I was talking about, but that he really didn't want to compete with other Native students for a "best" award. I could see that the other students were in silent agreement. "Would it be possible," Eddie continued, "for us to work with a famous Native writer?"

As we continued to talk a vision began to unfold. Instead of an annual award, we decided to find a way to link beginning and emerging Native student writers with established, published Native writers who would work together for a year in an Apprentice/Mentor relationship. The student apprentices would submit their writing to their assigned mentor who would critique the writing and send it back to the student. First and foremost was to keep the process as simple as possible.

In October, three months following the end of the Festival, the first invitations were sent to everyone attending the Returning The Gift Festival to participate as apprentices or mentors in a project that is now known as Wordcraft Circle of Native Writers and Storytellers.

Some six months later Wordcraft Circle Mentor (and National Caucus board member) D. L. (Don) Birchfield (*Choctaw*) accurately articulated the role of the Mentor to his Wordcraft Circle Apprentice. "Hopefully," Don wrote to his apprentice, "we'll be able to arrive at a comfortable level of exchange that will not be too burdensome for you, as I am here to try to be of assistance to you rather than become a new headache."

Three years later (November 1995), I can clearly see that Wordcraft Circle is much more than even I had imagined. The comments and letters of participants continue to surprise and delight me. "I am excited about participating in the Wordcraft Circle as a Mentor to help young writers and to pass on what I have learned." stated one Native mentor. Ruth Hall (*Hidatsa*), a high school Apprentice wrote that "Writing is a very vital part of my life. Participating in the project (Wordcraft Circle) will help me develop my writing technique." "I believe" said established Native writer Beth Brant (*Bay of Quinte Mohawk*), "the gift of writing carries the responsibility that extends throughout generations and I am anxious to have more Indian writing in the world."

All doubt vanished about the value of writing and the role of Wordcraft Circle with a letter from Ganuteyohi—or Glenn J. Twist— (*Cherokee/Creek*), a 76 year old (at the time) beginning Native writer who decided to become a Wordcraft Circle apprentice. In a long letter accompanying his application, he stated: ". . . I just have so much to write, that when I dry up in one area, I turn to another. This procedure has kept me busy and alive for five years." He continued in the following paragraph, "In a sense, I've been in a horse race with the final effects of lung cancer. What I don't get written will be lost forever, because I am the last person in my family to have the privilege of having heard the oral stories . . . Everything I have written so far must go through one more stage. . . . You ask why? I didn't have a mentor to tell me I should write in an organized manner. . . . Fact is, when I started writing, my only purpose was to stay alive. I was a green hand, no experience, no training, and no teaching. But, I have learned a lot since I started writing, mainly because people have gone out of their way to help me improve. I have been grateful for every suggestion I've received, even those I didn't accept. I have been very fortunate."

As we welcome more and more Native writers and storytellers into the circle, the vision which began to unfold that night in July 1992 becomes even stronger. There are more than 200 Native writers and storytellers now participating in Wordcraft Circle who range in age from 10 (currently the youngest) to 79 from 37 states and 3 countries representing more than 110 sovereign Native Nations. They are committed to the Wordcraft Circle vision "to ensure that the voices of Native writers and storytellers—past, present, and future—are heard throughout the world."

Since that first gathering of Native writers and storytellers at the Returning The Gift Festival, Native writers and storytellers participating in Wordcraft Circle continue to excel. Over the past two years (1993–1995), poetry written by Wordcrafters has been published in more than 60 collections of poetry. Over sixty books (poetry, prose—fiction and non-fiction—) written by Wordcrafters have been published. Wordcrafters have authored 51 essays, 48 articles, and 15 short stories which have been published in anthologies, journals, magazines and newspapers. Ten anthologies and six reference books have been edited or co-edited by Wordcrafters. Writings by Wordcrafters have been recorded on eleven audio-cassettes and four CD's. There have been ten plays and eleven TV/film scripts written by Wordcrafters. Finally, of the five Native authors who have been awarded the North American Indian Prose Award, three are Wordcrafters.

Of special importance are the accomplishments of Wordcraft Circle apprentices, most of whom attended the first Returning The Gift Festival. In July 1995, Glenn J. Twist, a Wordcraft Circle apprentice and Elder, who did not attend the Festival, became the fourth recipient of the Louis Littlecoon Oliver Memorial First Book Award for his prose (novel) manuscript, *Boston Mountain Tales* to be published by The Greenfield Review Press. Sadly, Glenn passed over in September 1995 before his book was actually published.

The young Choctaw high school student has graduated (as have so many others) and continues his participation as a Wordcraft Circle apprentice. Penny Olson is now teaching writing at a tribally controlled community college in Michigan and is a Wordcraft Circle Mentor to three Native writers. A poem which she wrote was published in the 1995 AISES (American Indian Science and Engineering Society) Conference Program. Eddie Webb is busy working on his Master's degree at the University of Arizona. Prior to continuing his academic program, he was with the Poets-In-The-Schools Program in California where he worked with beginning writers. He was also elected to the Wordcraft Circle National Caucus board for a two-year term.

Stuart Hoahwah (*Comanche/Apache*), a high school student who participated in the Festival, recently became a member of Wordcraft Circle as a Mentoring Core apprentice, some three years following the first Returning The Gift Festival. Currently attending the University of Arkansas at Little Rock, Stuart plans "to teach in higher education and to be a poet. . . . " In his application letter, Stuart says, ". . . what is important to me is the feedback on my work from a professional Native American writer. This will help me grow as a poet." He continues, "I want to break from [the] shell of shyness. I want my poetry to engulf many aspects of life and the Native American experience."

Stuart, like Penny, Eddie and other Wordcrafters, understands that in today's information age the skills of competent Native storytellers and writers are critically important because the leaders of today and tomorrow among the People of the sovereign Native nations must be able to effectively communicate orally and in writing. These new word-bringers understand that Native leaders must be able to write and tell stories which "teach and delight" and which promote understanding among all people so that the sovereign Native nations will continue to thrive and prosper.

This section focuses on the work of Wordcraft Circle which has continued following the first Returning The Gift Festival. For many Native students, their first encounter with the creative writing process usually occurs during their early years in school. For some, it is a wonderful experience. For others, it is incomprehensible because the writing exercises do not seem to have anything to do with their lives as Native people.

An important component of the Returning The Gift Festival was the opportunity for high school and college Native students to hear and talk with professional Native writers and storytellers. The importance of this strategy cannot be over-emphasized because through this process, Native students were able to have their fresh voices heard by those who come from a similar cultural mind-set. Also important is the manner in which knowledge is passed from elders (in this context, established Native writers and storytellers) to their younger relations in a non-confrontational manner.

To begin this section, the perspective of two well-established Native writers is presented. The first is by Abenaki poet Cheryl Savageau who was a presenter at the Returning The Gift Festival. Cheryl Savageau. In her quiet gentle way, she told the Festival participants that she had "heard from many Native writers that poetry starts in the body." To "find that power, to find that voice" with "the sound that comes to empower it" Cheryl suggested a few exercises "so that when the poem does come, you're ready for it." Because Native students attending the Festival and Wordcraft Circle Apprentices have found Cheryl's suggestions very helpful, it begins this section of the book.

A "Letter to an Apprentice Poet" by Cherokee author and Festival participant Charles Brashear follows Cheryl's presentation. To help beginning Native writers better understand what poetry is about, Charlie poses four important questions which he answers.

Choctaw author D. L. (Don) Birchfield gives some very practical pointers to prose writers in his essay, Advice To A Wannabe Professional Writer. Don is an active Wordcraft Circle Mentor who works with several beginning and emerging Native writers.

Cherokee traditional storyteller and Wordcraft Circle Mentor Gayle Ross presents her views on traditional storytelling including some important rules for the tellers of traditional stories.

Poet and novelist Sherman Alexie (*Spokane/Coeur d'Alene*) regularly works with young beginning and emerging Native writers on the reservation. A Wordcraft Circle Mentor, Sherman offers some important advice for those who are interested in the art of telling contemporary stories.

Concluding this section are practical tips for beginning and emerging Native writers who read their work in public by Wordcraft Circle Mentor Carol Lee Sanchez (*Laguna Pueblo*). A poet and essayist, Carol Lee ran the readings at the Coffee Gallery in San Francisco, California for many years. She was also the Director of the Poets-In-The-Schools program for the state of California.

Practical Advice When Writing Poetry

Cheryl Savageau (*Abenaki*)
Wordcraft Circle Mentor

I started to write poetry by accident. I went back to school after being away for about ten years and it was the only class I could take on the night I could get a baby-sitter. After about three or four weeks of writing, I found out that I was really hooked on it, that I could do it, and that I liked it.

I was very lucky to be living in Worcester, Massachusetts at the time, and there was a black poet named Ethridge Knight who started writing poetry when he was in prison. He started a poetry workshop in a little bar downtown for anyone who wanted to come—it was free. One of the things that Ethridge said to those of us who came to that workshop was that we did not have to write in the model that was out there—that academic model. What we needed to do was to listen to the voices of our own communities, and those voices would be the strength that would come through our poetry.

Another thing that he was convinced of—and this is something I have since heard from many Native writers as well—is that poetry starts in the body. It doesn't start with an idea so much as it starts with the body. Sometimes you might have an image in your mind that comes, or you might have a story you want to tell, but that story is not going to be the poem until you have the sound that comes to empower it. What I'd like to do a little bit of is to share some ways to find that power, to find that voice.

The first thing is to listen to the sounds of your body, to listen to your heartbeat, to listen to your breath. Your breath is what is going to connect you to the listener of your poem. Breath is spirit, so you can carry a lot of power in that way. So that your words will come from your heart, you go to the heart, not the brain. Not the mind. What makes your heart a listener is part of the responsibility and the power of being a poet.

Because I feel that sound is so important, one of the most important things for me in being a poet is listening. Different kinds of things that I listen to, first, I guess, is my own body because I live in it. Then I try to remember the voices of my childhood. I want to encourage all of you to think back to those voices that you heard when you were growing up. A lot of times, our very truest voice is the voice we grew up with, not the voice we might have learned later to get along in society (all those other voices get put on top of the first voice of our childhood.) A lot of very powerful poems can come out of experiences that you've had with your family, with your own childhood. With that voice, don't think of writing a poem. Write it down as if you were telling it to someone you loved that knew you as a child, and most likely that voice will begin to surface.

Another important thing is listening to the earth. Where I live is what's called New England now, in the Northeast. It's covered with trees where there aren't houses. It's a forest trying to come back. There's lots of water there. We have four seasons and the earth does speak to you if you're quiet enough to listen and to pay attention.

I'd like to tell you a few actual techniques that you can use to play with sound. First, let me say that the way I feel about technique is that what you want to do is to make your technique as conscious as possible. In other words, craft your sentence. But when you're really writing a poem, that's the time to forget about technique. When the real poem comes your subconscious knows all that and will use what it needs. You don't have to be thinking so much about it at the time you're writing it. Later, you can go back and revise and polish it up, but for that first voice, in order for it to be effective, forget about technique and just let the poem go through you.

I would like to suggest a few exercises that you can do so that when the poem does come, you're ready for it. One of the things that I did to make myself conscious of sound was to play with sound, to enhance different sounds myself, and try to square it with my body. And while all languages are different, most of them are made up of vowels and consonants. Vowel sounds are particularly important. They're the Ohs, the Ahs, the Eees and they carry a lot of power, a lot of spirit with them.

I just want to do a couple of those sounds with you. We'll just do one sound. You can do it at whatever pitch feels good to you. What I'd like to ask you to do while you're doing the sound is to pay attention to where you actually feel it in your body. Is it in your throat? Is it in your head? Is it in your belly? Is it in your back? See where you feel it, and also, pay attention to how it makes you feel. It is a good feeling? It is an energetic feeling? Is it a sad feeling for you? You can do this exercise with your eyes opened or closed—however you can best concentrate. Let's start with the sound Ah, and just do it at whatever is a natural voice for you.

Aaaaaaaaaaaaaaaaaaaaaahhhhhhhhhhhhhhhhh.

For me the sound is right there in my heart space. For other people it may be a slightly different place. Let's try a different sound. How about the sound Oh?

Oooooooooooooooooooohhhhhhhhhhhhhhhhhhh.

For me that sound goes much lower in my heart and I can feel a peacefulness that happens in my body when I hear that sound. I want to do one more sound with you. This is something you should try by yourself at home, not just with me telling you how it feels to me. Really pay attention to how it feels to you. Let's try the Eee sound.

Eeeeeeeeeeeeeeeeeeeeeeeeeeeeeeeeeeeeeeeeeeeee.

As we do all of those sounds you can feel there's a different kind of spirit that comes into the room. The sounds themselves are powerful.

If you remember how those sounds feel, then when you're writing a poem and you haven't got that sort of feeling and you want to put it across, you may find yourself wanting to do a lot of those sounds.

Again, for me, what is best is to make the technique as conscious as you can. Practice and do all kinds of exercises. However, when the poem comes, forget the exercises. Don't think about technique at all. That's all I have to say.

Letter to an Apprentice Poet

Charles Brashear (*Cherokee*)
Wordcraft Circle Mentor

I see from the samples you sent that you want and need to write poems, that you have had experiences that can make poems, that you have felt intensely and want to express and communicate your feelings. That I see that much already is a measure of your success. You're learning. To help you learn more, let me ask and then try to answer a few fundamental questions about poetry.

1. What do we want, when we write a poem?

We want the reader/listener to feel what we felt, understand what we understood, experience the experience that gave rise to our need to write the poem in the first place. A poem is a kind of sophisticated show-and-tell in which the poet's words generate an original, personal experience in the reader/listener. Since experience is the primary way any of us learns anything, a good poem is a re-created universe in which our experience happens for the first time to the reader/listener. When and if our experience is duplicated in the reader/listener's experience, then he/she feels what we feel, knows what we know. And that's exactly what we want—for the reader/listener to know what we know, feel what we feel.

2. What are poems made of?

Things. Things we can see, smell, touch, taste, hear, sense in some way. Only the sensory presentation of things is capable of becoming a reality in our reader/listener's mind. Because we are taught in school to explain poems, we tend to get the erroneous idea that they are made of emotions or ideas. But they aren't. They give rise to emotions and ideas. They fail if they don't give rise to emotions and ideas. But they are made of things, the sensory presentation of things. Emotions and ideas cannot be communicated directly. Only perceptions can be communicated directly. That's why we say, as in all arts, "Show, don't tell."

3. How do poems communicate?

With image, action, images-in-action—that is, anecdote or story—which enter into the reader/listener's experience and become his/her own.

You've probably heard that "experience is the best teacher" (actually it's the only teacher); well, the language of experience is the only way we have of making another person know what we know, feel what we feel, experience what we experience.

Be careful of assertion. Assertion is very weak in generating any experience in the reader/listener. It depends upon the reader/listener already having had a parallel experience, which he/she can substitute for the meaning at that point. When I say, above, that a poem is a form of show-and-tell, I'm depending upon your knowing what show-and-tell is . . . depending upon your having experienced show-and-tell. If you're a South Sea Islander who has never seen or heard of show-and-tell in American and European kindergartens, "show-and-tell" will be just so many baffling words. Your experience must overlap with my experience before my assertion can mean anything at all to you.

This means that assertion is limited to what has already passed, to what is already common knowledge; it is no good at all in creating new experiences. When we're buying fruit at the supermarket or giving directions to a stranger or collecting the rent, thank goodness for assertion. It's a kind of linguistic coin-of-the-realm, with which we conduct the business of everyday living; we depend upon other people knowing (approximately) what we mean when we talk. But what has already happened to (almost) everybody is not the stuff of poetry. And mere assertion is not the language of poetry.

The language of poetry is a language of image and experience . . . of images that become the reader/listener's experience. His/her experience, not yours. If you confess your personal experience to the reader, you will communicate exactly to the extent that his/her personal experience already parallels yours.

The grammar of most poetry is a language of comparisons . . . of similes, of metaphors, of allegories, of symbols (all are forms of comparison)—in all of which an image is substituted for an idea. You may say "I want to hide from the pressures felt inside." That's still at the level of mere assertion.

Let's substitute an image, an image involving pressure. "I want to hide from the balloon felt inside." Now the pressure felt inside is compared to something in almost everyone else's experience. But it's still vague. Like almost everyone else, I have felt balloons of happiness, balloons of fear, balloons of anger, balloons of frustration, etc. The line "I want to hide from the balloon felt inside" eliminates only one of the experiences I listed, for we usually don't want to hide from happiness. But it could be any of the others. Submerged in the line is a comparison: the pressure felt inside is like a balloon of (let's say) fear. Combining the image and the abstraction (balloon of fear) is a first step in making the abstraction into an experience.

When we write a poem, we try to find just exactly the right comparison to contain and communicate our experience. Let's try some other images of pressure: "I want to hide from the vise of frustration felt inside." "I want to hide from the fist of fear felt inside." (Got a little alliteration in that one!) "I want to hide from the tiger of anger felt inside." (Of course, tigers aren't pressure, but they're power and tension and danger that might substitute for pressure; that is, they are psychological pressure.) These comparisons are fairly easy, maybe even hackneyed, but as we push the language of our assertions into a language of comparisons we come closer and closer to what poetry is, closer and closer to evoking our experience in the reader/listener.

Our next step is to try to eliminate the abstraction; that is, try to find an image that contains both the balloon and the fear. "I want to hide from the fist inside." "I want to hide from the tiger inside." "My heart wants to hide from the feathers inside." "My heart hides from the talons inside." (That one might work, since your poem ends with "I am Eagle. Eagle looks down at me, protecting my spirituality," though you need an image to substitute for that vague abstraction, "protecting my spirituality"— maybe an image of motherly love, which is (let's say) protective and spiritual: "Eagle swaddles me gently in soft talons." "Eagle feathers my nest with talons." Yuck! Well, maybe those don't work, but I hope you get the idea: images that act on other images create experiences, which the reader perceives directly as his/her own experience. When that happens, the reader/listener enters into and experiences our poetry as if it were his/her own.

If that happens, all those other things that poets have traditionally worried about—meter, rhyme, assonance, alliteration, etc—become less important. Not unimportant, but of less importance. Poets have always thought of their craft as composed of two big parts—sound and sense. The poetry is in the sense, as I have tried to indicate above. But the "music," "the singing," the aesthetic element, is in the sound, which is to say, in the verse. Don't confuse verse with poetry. Verse is all sound; we identify it by sonic clues—meter, line-length, rhyme, stanza, etc. Excellent poetry can be written without verse, as has most "free verse" in the 20th century, though it may be harder to write "good" free verse than good poetry. And a great versifier can almost pass as a poet (e.g., Longfellow). As readers, we want both those qualities. When we read a poem, a good poem, we want to look up at a blank wall afterward and say to our inner self (1) Gulp! that was worth saying, and (2) Wow! that was well-said! And that's exactly what we want our readers to do with our poems.

Advice To A Wannabe Professional Writer

D. L. (Don) Birchfield (*Choctaw*)
Wordcraft Circle Mentor

Thank you for your last mailing. It's taken me longer than usual to get back to you because I've been printing out a book manuscript on my computer. I finally got the thing put in the mail, barely making my deadline.

I've had some things published since I wrote to you last, and I've enclosed copies of them. . . . I don't often receive letters from editors asking that I send them a story. I did not receive a letter of acceptance for it, which is also a bit untypical. I had no idea they had published it until I received my contributor's copies of the magazine (they sent me three copies, with a note that payment would follow at a later date, which *is* fairly typical).

. . . I have a copy of the *Chicago Manual of Style*. It was a $38 book, but I got it on a remainder table at a bookstore for $4. I think they've published a new edition since I got my copy. It's a big, thick book which is very tedious reading, dealing entirely with the process of converting typescripts into published material, mostly having to do with the various stages in the process of bookmaking. Many publishers follow the *Chicago Manual of Style*. As a writer, the more familiar you are with its contents—its do's and don'ts—the more professional your typescript will appear and the less editing it will require. I recommend that you take a look at a copy, which you can find in any decent library. A few minutes spent browsing through it will pay immediate dividends, and the more time you can spend studying it the more professional your typescripts will be. Editors at the better publishing houses and periodicals notice these things. They can spot an amateur typescript at one hundred yards, and believe me, they groan, because they know it will require a lot of editing if they are to publish it. This predisposes editors against the typescript before they begin to read it, if they even bother to do more than glance at the first few pages before sending it back (or dumping it in the trash if it didn't come with a self-addressed, stamped (SASE) return mailer).

I'm intentionally exaggerating things a bit here for the sake of making a point. You might publish for years, as I did, in the small presses, where the editors are as apt to have as little acquaintance with the *Chicago Manual of Style* as the average person. But if you're going to be a writer you'll encounter its requirements sooner or later, especially with book publishers. The sooner you become familiar with those requirements, the better off you'll be. By the same token, print journalists use the *Associated Press Style Manual* (or AP style manual), most university literary quarterlies use the *Modern Language Association Style Manual*, usually referred to simply as MLA, and the U. S. government has its own style manual for its publications. Some book publishers, such as McGraw-Hill, have their own style manual and many professions have one, such as the style manual used only by professional psychology journals. Each manual is different, especially regarding the style of footnote citations, but also for many other things. The government manual, for example, has about fifty some odd pages dealing only with hyphens. The greater variety of writing you do, the greater variety of style manuals you'll need to be familiar with, because if you type your manuscript in the style used by a particular publication or profession it will require less editing. If you used the *Turabian Style Manual* for college history research papers, you might be interested to know that it is a condensation of the *Chicago Manual of Style*.

If this all sounds terribly complex, don't be too worried about it right now. I'm just telling you about some things you need to be aware of and that you need to begin looking into. You might keep it in the back of your mind when you are browsing in used bookstores or college bookstores. The latest edition of the AP style manual, for example, is always for sale in the community college bookstore near my home because it is a required purchase for the students taking Journalism 1, and they offer that class every school term. The style manuals don't ordinarily change very much from one edition to the next, so if you see one in a used bookstore you can pick it up pretty cheap. I've acquired a number of different manuals that way. At odd moments I sometimes compare their differences, which can be an education in itself.

. . . I have had things published that range through just about the entire spectrum of editing. I once made a simultaneous submission of an essay to a number of different state chess journals. A lot of them published it. One editor practically rewrote the entire essay, introducing a number of grammatical errors, I might add, whereas one editor published a photo reduction of my double-spaced typescript. The same essay, two different editors. When I send a manuscript out I never know how much of it will end up in print, unless I receive galley proofs. Having been an editor myself I know that an editor frequently doesn't know how much of a manuscript will actually be published until the very last minute when it comes time to try to fit the free-lance editorial content into the space available, after the advertising, regular features, etc., have gone in. The closer the publication comes to being of a journalistic nature, the more this will be the case.

I hope these experiences of mine will give you some idea of what to anticipate when you begin submitting material for publication, especially if you submit writings to a wide variety of different kinds of publications, as I do. Remember that studies have shown that the most experienced copy-editor will only catch about 85% of the errors in a manuscript. There is a direct correlation between the number of errors in the original type-script and the number of errors that end up appearing in print. So to look as good as you can in print, submit a typescript as error free as you can make it.

Good luck with this adventure!

The Art of Traditional Storytelling

Gayle Ross (*Cherokee*)
Wordcraft Circle Mentor

I have some feelings that have evolved over my 15 years telling stories as a performance art form. At the same time, I am very conscious of my place in an ongoing tradition that is very important to our Native culture. We, who are Native tellers, even if we adapt to make a profession out of it and perform in many different venues, always have to be mindful of the fact that we are participating, or hopefully are participating in an ongoing tradition that has been vital to our cultural survival. We tell out of a tradition, if we tell our own traditional material, that stretches back thousands of years and these stories are essential to our understanding of ourselves as Indian people.

Everything about our culture was transmitted in story form and if you talk to such great Indian writers like N. Scott Momaday (*Kiowa*), Leslie Silko (*Laguna Pueblo*), or Susan Power (*Lakota*), they will tell you that at the heart of everything they write—which is Native American literature—is their own particular tribal oral traditions.

Equally important is that we need to be always mindful of the fact that we are a bridge between past and present, between present and future, between our culture and the dominant culture. If we're approaching traditional storytelling correctly, then being a bridge is uppermost in our hearts. This entails a certain level of responsibility to the community from which we come and a certain level of responsibility to the non- Indian community that listens to us. They come to us hoping to learn something about the Indian community.

Which brings me to some "rules" concerning the different areas of storytelling traditions. Rules such as: which nations had traditions of telling seasonally; which nations had traditions that meant only certain people could tell certain stories. You walk a very fine line between balancing respect for those traditions and the needs of this culture that we find ourselves in now.

Whenever possible I try to find out enough to know and be comfortable with telling a story from another tribe. Usually that entails a personal relationship with someone from that tribe who I have respect for as a tradition keeper. If I don't have that kind of relationship, then I won't tell that story. When I have established a personal relationship with someone from another tribe, I try to follow everything they teach me about the story. I learn about whether it should be told at a certain time of year, or a certain time of day, or whether I'm the person to tell it at all. The majority of Indian tellers that I know and have heard haven't violated the rules of a tribe from which the story comes. I don't mean to sound separatist, but if somebody comes out of a tradition of telling these stories, they are almost always predisposed to understand that they need to know a lot before they can be a responsible keeper for the spirit of the story.

There are Native storytellers who have come up with some creative solutions to balancing their traditional responsibilities and their need to make a living in this society. Jeri Keems, a wonderful Navajo storyteller, discussed the situation with several Navajo elders. They agreed that it was more important for her to be able to teach about Navajo culture, through the stories than it was for her to follow the traditional Navajo restrictions against telling in the summer. So Jeri tell stories in the summer because she's been given permission to do so.

At the same time, I have very strong feelings about people from outside the Native culture telling the stories. And while I have given permission to non-Indian tellers to use some of the material that I use, it's because they are people who have a good understanding of Native history and where we come from and the stories are about all of us as humans, like the rabbit stories and trickster stories. That aside, my strong feelings stem from the observation that for too many years our stories have been perverted either by well-meaning or not well-meaning non-Indians.

We've been told that ethnologists, anthropologists, language specialists, folklorists that they know more about us than we do. And I reject that notion out of hand. The first step in cultural sovereignty, to me, is insisting on the right to define ourselves by our music, by our dance, by our writing, and by our storytelling. It means the dominant society has to step back and let us tell our own story. In that sense, in my view, we do have special knowledge when it comes to ourselves.

Sadly this is something that you often cannot or is very difficult to get across to many non-Indian tellers. With the exception of people who come to live with us, and immerse themselves in the culture for years, like Richard Erdoes, non-Indian storytellers too often insist that they are being very respectful while they cheerfully make changes that obliterate the essence of the story. They will tell you that they are feeling very respectful as they are doing this. However, in the Indian tradition, you don't feel respect, you act with respect. To me it's not a racial issue but rather as a cultural one.

Native storytellers must walk the same fine line. Those of us who publish and those of us who perform must always be vigilant when it comes to making changes to a traditional story. We must think very carefully about the changes we are asked to make. Where do we draw the line? What should we do if a traditional story says " . . . and then somebody came along and saw that it was the giant spirit dog" and your editor says to you, "couldn't that somebody be a little boy, it would be nice to have a little boy character in this story."

To me, a change like this to a traditional story is relatively harmless. The story already says "somebody came along" but when your editor says to you, "well I really am nervous having seven menstruating women defeat the power of this giant, couldn't it be that . . . " then I feel you must say "No. No. I'm sorry. That's too essential a part of the story to mess with. That goes in like it is or you don't get the story."

Another point I want to make to tellers of traditional stories is not to be tempted to manipulate for audience response or greed. If you develop a certain degree of skill or dedication, or if you live long enough, sooner or later somebody will be at your side trying to appeal to your greed.

In many ways we must always keep in mind that these stories live on the breath. Even if you write them down and publish them and make them live beautifully, I believe our first and foremost responsibility is to the story and to the way it lives on the breath and in the minds and hearts of the people who hear the story.

Finally, I want to encourage more people to investigate telling stories. I think that when someone is a keeper of a traditional story, when someone has that spirit in their care, there is no more powerful sharing that is possible. In my view, it is one of the best ways to teach.

The Art of Contemporary Storytelling

Sherman Alexie (*Spokane/Coeur d'Alene*)
Wordcraft Circle Mentor

My father was always a storyteller, not in the traditional sense, but he was constantly telling stories about the way he grew up, about the people in our family, and our friends and the people in the tribe. I was always exposed to somebody who could tell a story that was funny. As Indian people, we are constantly exposed to storytelling from the time we are small children but we just don't think "contemporary" storytelling would appeal to a non-Indian audience.

Actually, the kinds of stories my dad told were pretty much the same kind of stories I write now. What I have learned is that small ordinary things can make an incredible story. Until I started reading Indian writers I didn't know that you could write a poem or a story about fry bread, or about going to a powwow, or about even waking up in the morning. I never realized how simple a story could be. That's why my stories are about ordinary lives and the things we do everyday.

Because storytelling is what I do and what I've always done with my work, when I am writing it, I read it aloud constantly. So, even as I'm creating it on the page for the very first time, I'm also reading it aloud to myself, seeing how the stories and poems sound. By the time I get to actually telling a story, I've heard it so many times and said it aloud so many times to myself that I think my actually telling the story is a lot more effective. Stories and poems, even if they're on the page, are still about sound. We have to remember that and keep reading them aloud.

Many beginning and emerging storytellers place so much pressure on themselves to tell these grand stories with huge morals or to present larger-than-life messages. I think this originated with reading Shakespeare and so for many storytelling seems to be all about huge dramatic events. As a result, when we Indian people start telling our stories, we tend to start thinking that we need to make these huge political statements about being Indian, or about oppression, or about politics.

What I've learned is that if it's a simple story, and if it's a good story, all those things will be in it anyway, and we don't need to force feed it. It's our individual lives that will make our stories ring true to people. There's no need to try to be generic. It's what has happened to us specifically, it's what we know about specifically, that will make us able to tell good stories.

I would strongly encourage beginning storytellers who are in high school to get involved in any kind of public speaking they can, whether it's debate or extemporaneous speaking, or student government or anything like that. When you're in high school there are so many opportunities to get over the fear of public speaking and storytelling. For adults, it's difficult to even begin to think about changing their lives and taking on the challenges of public speaking.

When you first get up in front of a crowd and speak, it's a lot easier when you didn't write the material. That's why I recommend that high school students get involved in debating. In debate, you're not necessarily getting emotionally involved. You're not talking about your poems or your stories. You're talking or arguing a certain point. The important point is that you are able to become comfortable when speaking to an audience. Learning to be comfortable when speaking before an audience is going to help when you become a storyteller of your own material or of other material in which you are emotionally involved.

For those in college who are interested in becoming good storytellers, I would suggest that you set up your own readings at the local coffee shop. This is what my friends and I did when I was in college. Sometimes there would be five people in the audience. Sometimes 50. It varied. But that wasn't important. What mattered was that we were constantly reading our material. We were continually practicing our material in front of groups of people. We would critique each other and we'd say "well you should do this" or "you should do that" or "we didn't like that." By doing this, we sharpened our storytelling skills. I really think one of the best things to do is bring together a group of people whose opinions you trust. People you think are serious about their craft and do a lot of readings together. Do one a month in the area you're from and don't worry about whether there's going to be a crowd or not.

I've also found that when you're advertising your readings, promoting yourself and setting up space, you're making much more of a commitment to the art of storytelling. Too often, we decide to stay in our rooms and write because we're afraid to go out there and do anything with our stories. But, if you're forced to promote yourself, your work, your storytelling, then I think it becomes much more emotionally involving and you become much more active publicly.

By taking advantage of the opportunities for speaking in public even if it means creating your own opportunities, the end result is that you will be able to tell good "contemporary" stories which your audiences will applaud.

The Performing Poet As An "Almost" Storyteller

Carol Lee Sanchez (*Laguna Pueblo*)
Wordcraft Circle Mentor

The person who is a natural extemporaneous speaker can stand before a group of people and recite poetry with such ease that he can spell-bind an audience immediately into loving poetry, even though they didn't particularly care for it before. These rare exceptions give many of us who don't seem to have that ability the idea that we can't compare—can't possibly do what they do and so should not attempt it.

There are also poets/writers who feel they can do just as well as the spellbinding type of speaker and even if they can't, they want to be heard so they read their works in public anyway. The hard truth about many oral poets is their inability to entertain and hold an audience's attention past the first poem.

Most untrained readers have a deadly sing-song style of reading in a monotonous tone that is guaranteed to put an audience to sleep in a very short time. Some, trying to be dynamic readers, start out in a booming voice and yell their entire reading in the same monotone—but at full volume. You can't go to sleep, but you can become bored very quickly because there is no variety.

An audience needs variety in a performance in order to become engaged with the work presented. Engagement permits emotional participation with the work and leaves a lasting impression with the participants which benefits both the performer and the listener. And while this is true for all types of public performances, traditional as well as contemporary storytellers are well aware of this special interaction. Poets, on the other hand, often forget to honor their own words or have never thought about their words as objects to be honored.

My own journey from reading my poems in a breathy monotone into a microphone on the stage of the Coffee Gallery in San Francisco in 1966, to becoming a performing poet, co-founder of The Order of the Blue Scarf, and state-wide director of the California Poets-In-The-Schools (CPITS) program, has been a rewarding one. It has been a learning experience for me. What is also true is that I continue to learn something new each time I give a reading.

Reading my poems aloud to an audience was (and still is) more important to me than having them in print. There are several reasons for this but I suspect the most compelling one has to do with my Native Laguna Pueblo heritage and upbringing. Although I am bi-racial, I am also multi-cultural by race *and* ethnicity. As a result, I grew up with quite a few linguistic rhythms and forms of oral presentations from conversational dialogues to dramatic performances. As a descendant of a tribal culture with a rich oral tradition, it seems quite natural that I would choose to perform in public.

Among Native Indian cultures, the oral tradition is still practiced in Native languages during tribal ceremonies. Native performances tend to focus on the metaphysical (non-visible) connections between humans and the rest of nature. It is a celebration of human survival and thanksgiving to all things benefitting humans. Native oral tradition is about being mindful in all endeavors and to treat all things, including self, as sacred and worthy of respect. I say this because I believe performing can be related to the general principles of celebration of spirit, revival, respect, and mindfulness.

In my view, the skills of a performing poet lie somewhere between the techniques of an actor and that of a traditional storyteller. The poet is presenting a personal perspective about a personal experience. A traditional storyteller is, in the main, interpreting the words and ideas of another. As a poet, whether published in books or "in performance", my objective is to present my unique vision to as large an audience as possible. When presenting my work to an audience, I draw on and consciously use the oral traditions of my multicultural and multilingual background to share my "little stories," my poems, with as many people as I can. I like to see my audience. I want to feel their responses, their connection with my thoughts and word choices, my form of presenting, and I want to hear their feed-back after a reading.

Some of the things I have learned along the way might be helpful to the poet/writer who decides to present their work in public. These insights are what I call the "nitty-gritty" how to's—some of the uncomfortable stuff we are reluctant to say out loud to each other. These points helped me develop my performing style and to "clean up" my breathy monotone about twenty years ago.

First, to help you discover your performing style, tape record yourself telling children's stories you "know by heart" such as "Goldilocks and The Three Bears" or "The Three Little Pigs" followed by a reading of four or five typed pages of favorite poems you have written.

Next, listen to the tape recording carefully and make notes of the differences between the two forms of oral presentation. Generally, the stories will sound more lively and animated. They will be more interesting because your voice will rise and fall in volume and become excited or scary or angry or sad depending on what's happening in the story. The poems you have read will tend to sound flat if they are read much like a story often sounds flat when being read from a book. You may notice a kind of sing-song style that gets monotonous. You may be reading too fast to be understood or you may be swallowing your word endings, not enunciating words clearly enough to be understood, or dropping your voice at the end of every line.

Next, think about honoring your words. After you have thought about this for a couple of minutes, read the same poems into the tape recorder again. Because you are conscious about honoring your words, you will know what to look for to help you give a better reading. Maybe it's to slow down, or speak a little louder. Vary the way you use your voice throughout a poem. Try reading a poem as though you are angry, or sad, or very happy, or frightened. Mix them up in the same poem. Experiment with your intonations, inflections, volume—go from a whisper to a shout. Sing a line or two into the tape recorder.

Practice reading in front of a mirror. Look up from the page at your reflection in the mirror then back down again without losing your place or the smoothness of the presentation. If you are reading at the appropriate speed for a listener to understand your thoughts, you can easily look up, then back to the page, and you won't stumble or lose your place. Now tape record yourself doing all of that while also facing the mirror as though you are the audience. Notice whether you are standing at ease or are bobbing and weaving or fidgeting when you read. Notice your unconscious "tics" and habits like scratching your nose often or rubbing your forehead or chin when you pause to get to the next thought, and so forth. Some unconscious mannerisms are enhancing to a person, others are very distracting and take the listener's attention away from the work. This leads me to: Thinking about honoring your audience.

It is the performer's duty to honor the audience. Once the spotlight illuminates the performer, it is the performer's job to entertain the listeners. It is the duty of performing poets to treat themselves, their words and their audience with respect. When people in the audience are falling asleep, the poet has lost their interest in some way. In my view, if the poet was honoring the audience and giving a dynamic performance, this wouldn't happen.

Prepare your reading. Choose the poems you want to read. Time your reading to fit the time alloted for which you have been scheduled. Ten minutes means ten minutes . . . not fifteen or twenty-five or thirty! Don't use precious time hunting for a poem or explaining each poem before you read or present it. It is inordinately unfair to take up time hunting for and/or explaining your poems. A brief introduction about the setting or in-spiration of a poem is fine if it is kept to thirty or forty seconds; it should rarely go over a minute. If the poem doesn't explain itself or illuminate the listener, then it doesn't work. That's how the poet finds out if the poem is communicating or not. Over-explaining takes away from the poem itself and the reading of it is anti-climatic (i.e., it let's the audience down). Time your reading long before you give it. This can be done at home when you have plenty of time to pick and choose your poems. Arrange them in the order you want to read them and time the whole reading.

Finally, I would suggest you get together with several other poets in your community and read aloud to each other in a semi-formal setting. The emphasis is to develop performance techniques which *only* includes feed-back about body movement, audience contact, voice inflection, enunciation, reading too fast, not projecting the voice, and sing-song, flat or monotonous recitation. Do not critique each other's poems. That should be reserved for a poetry writing workshop or session.

Keep in mind that you can memorize your poems, and if you do, you can present them in a much freer manner because you won't be hampered with holding a book or a piece of paper. But, if you don't feel comfortable with memorization, for whatever reason, you can still become a fine per-forming poet.

These are just a few suggestions that can help you develop your own unique style. Naturally, the more you read in public the better you will be-come. The better you become, the more comfortable you will be. Once you're comfortable on stage, you will communicate that comfort automat-ically to your audience and they will look forward to hearing you again and again. That's when you know you've become a performing foet—and an "almost storyteller." That doesn't mean you ever lose the "butterflies in the stomach" feeling, it just means that you've become an entertaining poet and people will love to listen to you read and perform you own work.

ANTHOLOGY OF EMERGING NATIVE VOICES

CELEBRATING THEIR VOICES

James Bruchac (*Abenaki*)

Recently, while preparing some promotional information for *Indian Artist Magazine*, I was reminded of an interesting piece of literary history. At the time I was putting together a list of Native-authored titles which The Greenfield Review Press had published over the last three decades. I felt it was important to list one of our first Native titles, *Laguna Woman*, published in 1975. This title, now long out of print, was the first book ever published by the then little-known Leslie Marmon Silko.

"Wow! What I great selling point!" I thought while happily adding this information to my promotional letter. Then, after lifting my fingers from the keyboard, I thought about all the Native authors we had published in anthologies and individual collections. Over the years we have published such authors as Ted Palmeteer, Paula Gunn Allen, Linda Hogan, Peter Blue Cloud, Lance Henson, Louis Littlecoon Oliver, Joy Harjo, James Welch, Robert J. Conley, N. Scott Momaday, Gerald Vizenor, Maurice Kenny, Wendy Rose, Carroll Arnett, and a host of others. Many, like Leslie Marmon Silko, were, at the time of publication, unknown writers with vast artistic talent.

Thinking further, I thought of the North American Native Authors First Book Awards, another outcome of the 1992 Returning The Gift Festival. Every year since 1992 hundreds of unpublished Native authors have submitted their manuscripts of poetry and fiction for this award. Winners in the poetry category have been published by The Greenfield Review Press, giving us the privilege of publishing Native poets such as Gloria Bird, Kimberly Blaeser, Tiffany Midge, Denise Sweet and recent fiction winner Glenn J. Twist. Choosing winners for these awards, however, seems to become more and more difficult every year with many deserving first place and even more that are close seconds.

Parenthetically, as assistant director of The Greenfield Review Press and as a writer, I feel a strong sense of pride and appreciation for the abundance of well-written Native literature published by us within the last three decades.

Since the original Returning The Gift Festival, the amount of quality Native literature, especially written by a younger generation, appears to be on the rise. This strikes a special note in my heart as the newly elected President of Wordcraft Circle of Native Writers & Storytellers. As President of Wordcraft Circle one of my primary goals is to continue to increase the number of young people in our Mentoring program. This combines with our organization's overall goal of getting more young people writing and eventually published. Since 1992, many have benefitted from such outreach programs at the Returning The Gift Writer Workshops, and now, from Wordcraft Circle.

The following is a sample of such work. These writings were selected from various Returning The Gift Writer Workshops and through Wordcraft Circle's Mentoring program. Within this section are works of poetry such as "On The Wings of an Eagle" by Evie Michelle Sunnyboy, which celebrates the many gifts of Native heritage. There is also Doreen Lee Deaton's poem, "Between Two Worlds," which speaks of the confusion of being of mixed descent. There are also short lesson stories such as "The Father, Son, and Donkey" by Willie Sanchez. Faith Allard's "Grandma Knows" combines the lessons of elders with contemporary issues. Whatever their message, the young writers express themselves well in a variety of ways, touching on a diversity of subjects and concerns.

Looking at these writings, I can't help but notice how far Native literature has come over the last three decades. Literally dozens of new Native writers have been published (and some even born) since The Greenfield Review Press published *Laguna Woman* in 1975. And while the young writers may not all be the next Leslie Marmon Silko, N. Scott Momaday, Joy Harjo, or Sherman Alexie, they, like those of generations before, have chosen to affirm themselves and their Native heritage through writing. They have chosen to write, to find a voice; a voice not only for their generation, but, like the goal of this anthology, to help inspire those yet to come.

RETURNING THE GIFT FESTIVAL STUDENT SCHOLARSHIP PARTICIPANTS

50 Ft. Deer

Shirley Brozzo

Driving down Hwy 41
See deer
too late
splat.

Don't stop
to say I'm sorry

Don't stop
to offer a prayer

Don't stop
to ask forgiveness

Don't stop

Driving down Hwy 41
See deer
everywhere
mailboxes
clumps of grass
small trees.

Last night
saw deer
50 ft tall
Huge trees
in the U.P.

Grandfather's spirit
tells me

Stop
to say I'm sorry

Stop
to offer a prayer

Stop
to ask forgiveness

Stop

No more
50 ft deer
on Hwy 41

January 30th Sea Lion Encounter

E. K. (Kim) Caldwell

rainbow arched in a charcoal sky
   resting with her tip swirling in the ocean
rock island holds her up
   waves crash and rise
   wrapping themselves around her edges

head to the beach
   heart singing
gentle rains from january sky
   wind speaks softly

and then there she was

beached and heaving weakly
   crying only when there was enough breath
between the shudders that moved through her

the look in her eyes
   her death chant close in her throat
the look in her eyes
   beyond panic now
      one weak bark
      eyes squeezed shut with the effort

tears blurring vision
   speaking to her
   making promises
more for myself than to her

knowing grandmother would take her
   as the tide washed in
and cradle her once more
   in a place so cold
      that the spirit is warmed.

rain pelting now
   tiny needles
then larger splashing drops
   mixing with tears
feeling helplessness in grandmother's presence
      knowing she will take her own
    in her own time
  it is not unfair
it is the way of the circle.

raining   pouring now
facing west into the wind
   offering prayers for her
   as she leaves for her journey

the look in her eyes
   ho! the look in her eyes.

Wampanoag Indian Museum of Mashpee, Massachusetts

Christopher Fleet

Can I tell you there was no lightening,
no wind to talk the trees into whispers.

It was more like over the hills and through the woods
to a salt box house I came,
the music playing everywhere except the background . . .
one little . . . two little . . . three little . . .

And the three women telling the story
of we can't remember,
looking like the sisters of Jimmy Hendrix,

The whole time catching my eye
long enough to throw it back
out the door.

I ran with smoke
back to upstate, NY
shredding the "Algonquin Umbrellas,"
an umbrella one old Hendrix sister told a Quebecois,
"kept our little Iroquois brothers safe at night."

Can I tell you there were cracks
all over the I-90, just below the Adirondacks,
where Mohawk blood beneath my feet
sucked in hard whispers from pine trees.
Did I tell you
we were never a people to forget.

Grandma Boyd

Ruth Ann Hall

Teetering grey towers of outdated news
encircle us like a protective mother's arms—
Hazy yellow light
hangs lazily above our heads—

Grandma's oxygen machine
monotonously moans muffled, mechanical complaints
that go unnoticed—
Bubba, Sally, and Henry
sniff rusty orange carpet
for comfortable nap spots—

Grandma leisurely chews frybread I made.
Her stories slowly begin to tumble out
over thin chapped lips in a proud parade
gaining momentum and fluidity.

Through Grandma's eyes: lush bottomlands,
succulent wild fruits and berries,
delicious wild potatoes and turnips,
clear water-narrow Missouri River,
one big extended Family living in the valley.

Through her ears: children's high pitched laughter,
the abundant leaves whispering in the wind,
stories visitors and guests animate,
Pa home at lunch singing with his hand drum.
Elbowoods, a time of work and simple happiness is remembered.

Old, expressive hands
covered in wrinkled brown flesh
unfold Grandma White Duck's
brilliant Purple wool shawl.

Through dime size moth holes:
My grandmother—
a skinny young girl—
dark downcast eyes—
obedient listening ears—
tiny ankles that don't stretch the elastic
in her white anklets.

Her Grandfather—a quiet gentle man—
cornsilky fine, brown hair
that was to be trimmed with long sharp scissors
by Grandma's young
inexperienced hands.
his hand-rolled cigarettes lined
in a perfect row on his crate furniture.

The greatest challenge—
a game of checkers—
at which he would always win.
But, one time,
even though he looked the board over
with extreme care,
Grandma was stealthy enough
to jump him
five times in a row
and win
a single game.

The East side of the house shelters
escaping hot, afternoon's summer Sun—
she sits with Grandma White Duck and Lone Woman
dark skinned Grandmothers
in high top moccasins
with long peppery braids
sprawled down calico dresses
tell stories and gossip
in their only tongue—Hidatsa.

In her office chair,
at the head of her round kitchen table,
She is almost finished
with her third piece of frybread
the remnants of her fried potatoes
are cleaned off her plate
with her last corner of bread.
Grandma folds the remaining frybread
in a protective blanket
of thin, shiny aluminum foil.

Grandma's long fingernails
scratch a picture
on a white styrofoam container:
their Home,
many visitors with in open welcome,
a straw bed topped
with many warm quilts
for Grandma White Duck.

My Brother and Sister

Donna John

My brother and sister
are dear and precious to me
Alcohol
separates us
like the Great Wall of China

Our Ancestors go back centuries
our blood
our ways
still remain

Alcohol powerful,
baffling,
and cunning
like the grim reaper stole my family

Every day I pray
the suffering will end
and we will be close again

Through the years
alcohol has distanced us
I search the streets of Fairbanks
hoping they will be sober
so we can talk

Sometimes I find them
they say, "I love you"
I say, "I love you"
We share our true heart
and it is enough.

Colors That Heal

Penny J. Olson

"In a healing circle all participants take turns talking. When someone is talking, everyone else should be listening. No one should interrupt the speaker." Jan had asked Nate what happened in a healing circle before he had left her office yesterday. "Listeners may nod in agreement, or say yes if they agree with the speaker, but if they disagree they should remain silent. Everyone gets a chance to speak. Never say anything negative about a previous speaker; just voice your opinion about the topic." Nate looked at Jan, and she nodded to show she understood. He then continued, "Steve will be the leader of this circle and will direct the topics we will be speaking about. If you don't want to speak you don't have to. Speak only if you feel comfortable or have something you want to say."

The twinge in Jan's stomach was gone, and she reclined a little more in her chair. She listened to what Steve said and concentrated only on that. For the first time since Monday, Jan forgot not only about the fight with Anita but about all the insecurities Anita's comments had raised concerning herself.

"Red is the color of the East," Steve said in a quiet comforting voice, which flowed in a steady almost hypnotic, rhythm. "It stands for the red race of man, or the Indian." Jan found herself thinking about the stories that Nate had been telling to her children lately. Most of them dealt with beginnings. She got as much enjoyment out of them as Jen and Jimmy did. She discovered Steve smiling at her. "All life begins with the color red. Each new day begins in the East and the east wind gives new life to our mother, the earth, in the spring. Everything begins again in the spring." Steve stood up, held a red piece of felt in his hands, and looked around the circle. "Animals have their young in the spring, and we begin to grow food. We also use animals for food. There is a relationship between food and feelings. Good food brings good feelings. When we feel good about ourselves we enjoy life and vision. This is the good part of the color red."

Jan looked around the circle; people barely breathed; they were so caught up in what Steve was saying. Steve held up a yellow piece of felt and started speaking again.

"Yellow is the color of the South. It represents, the Oriental race of people. It is also a symbol of time, relationships, and the sun. Yellow helps us to understand self through family, extended family, friends and community." Jan thought of her children again. Yellow was her daughter's favorite color. It fit her; Jen was so concerned with others' feelings. "Self-development is an important time for the young. We learn and understand ourselves through relationships. Relationships are the strength of color yellow." Steve was quiet as he held up a piece of black felt.

"Black is the color of the West. It represents the Black race of man. It also represents respect, reason, and water. Respect means to look twice at everything we do. The quality of our inner lives is enriched when we understand and use respect and reason."

Maybe that's it, Jan's mind raced through a maze of ideas. I'm angry and I can't reason when I'm angry. Maybe I'm giving my anger too much respect. Maybe I'm . . .

"White is the color of the North. It represents the Caucasian or the White race of Man." Steve's voice cut through to Jan. "It is a strong color since it is the symbol of caring, movement and air." Steve touched the piece of felt to his cheek. "Without caring, the other good feelings will wither and disappear. Caring is usually defined by how we interact with family, school, and community."

"Last is the color green." Steve put down the white piece of felt and gingerly picked up the green piece.

The power of his words reminded Jan of the time she had thrown a candy wrapper on the ground in front of her grandmother and walked away. Grandy went over to Jan, grabbed her by the hand, walked her back to the small Brach's candy wrapper, and made her pick it up. Jan always remembered Grandy telling her, "If we want Mother Earth to take care of us, we have to give her the respect she deserves. Look at all she has given us. Do you really think she deserves you covering her beautiful green floor with your thoughtlessness?"

Steve's voice reached out to Jan, "Green is a very important color because it is a healing color and the symbol for the Mother Earth. It is also a symbol of balance and listening. For these reasons, green is located in the center of the circle."

Steve picked up all the pieces of felt and continued speaking. "The spiritual principles of honesty and kindness are found in all the colors. All the colors are equal in strength beauty, and the harmony they bring to the

Mother Earth. No one color outweighs any of the others in importance to the well-being of mankind. I will pass these swatches around the circle now, and when they come to you, tell what color feels good for you at this time."

The first time around, Jan passed. She felt positive about more than one color and the memories they brought her. She also wasn't sure if she could say more than one color or not. Instead, she listened, and found herself amazed by what was going on around the circle. Karen talked about how she had always found the color green was there to listen to her problems even if no other human beings were. Nate told about the strength he discovered in the color yellow and relationships when he felt that nobody should have cared. The sharing that occurred helped Jan to heal as much as what Jan was discovering about herself.

The second time around, Steve explained the negative feeling involved with each color. Red had to do with feeling inferior. Ever since the day Jan and Anita had fought, her feelings of inferiority had gotten the better of her. Not only did she let it affect her professionally, but personally, emotionally, and intellectually as well. When Anita questioned who Jan was, based only on her appearance, it sparked some of Jan's own doubts. Once her own fears surfaced it seemed like the negative side of all the other colors joined in with the inferior feeling of red. Before Jan even realized it, she felt the envy of the yellow, the resentment of the black, and the jealousy of the green enter her life. She saw how even the not-caring of the white played a part in her life.

"Do I understand feeling inferior!" Jan said when she received the color swatches. She picked out the red one and laid it on her left thigh. "The problem is when I feel this way, all the negative emotions take over my life completely, not only the feeling of inferiority, but those feelings of envy, resentment, and jealousy. Because someone voiced my worst concerns about myself, I began believing they were true." Jan's words came rushing out as she began to relax. She stopped playing with the pieces of felt that Mark had handed to her, and picked up the white swatch. "However, I don't think I have ever stopped caring completely, no matter how much I may have wanted to. My anger wouldn't let me." She paused before continuing in almost a whisper. "Except about myself, maybe."

She passed the colors on to Nate, who had been sitting next to her. The gentle pressure of Nate's hand as he squeezed Jan's seemed to give Jan the strength she needed to continue.

After the colors made it around the second time, Steve told about the

fire that is found within each individual and how every person is in charge
of their own fire.

"The fire is found in the color green, because it is found in the center
of each person. Each person is responsible to tend their own fire and when
we forget this, we allow our fires to go out." While Steve talked, Jan
looked out the window at the sea gulls. She realized she had stopped tending her fire and had left it in Anita's care. This allowed Anita to make her
feel inferior. When it was her turn to talk, she felt at ease. She spoke up
honestly and openly.

"I realize what the majority of my problem is," she began quietly and
slowly. "I let all my insecurities found in the red take over. Before I knew
it, they turned into jealousy and anger. I allowed this person's opinions to
destroy what I believed to be good about me. I lost who I was. The only
thing that kept me going was my anger. I stopped looking within, to what
I know to be the truth for the answers. Instead I accepted her answers so I
wouldn't have to follow the path." She took a deep breath and released the
air naturally instead of forcing it out like she had been doing for the last
few days. The negative emotions of the others colors joined in and overwhelmed me. I was afraid to ask others for help. If nothing else has become clear to me today, I realize that it was me and only me, who stopped
tending my fire. I stopped caring, and allowed it to burn out." Jan looked
at Nate. "I can accept help from others in tending my fire, but it is up to
me to keep it burning at all times."

Jan smiled at Nate. He smiled back and shook his head yes. The
peace settling over her was complete. Whatever happened with Anita on
Monday would happen. Jan knew that she wasn't going to allow this
woman to make her question herself anymore. She would continue working with Indian students who were her clients. Anita no longer mattered.
Even though there were no guarantees about how long this feeling would
last, she now knew that if it didn't she could find her way back to it.

On the Wings of an Eagle

Evie Michelle Sunnyboy

On the wings of an eagle,
I am wild and free,
free from the worries that are troubling me,
I can see the present, past and the future,
I can tell what is coming and know what to expect.

On the wings of an eagle,
The choices are mine,
I have the responsibility to take care of myself,
To depend on the way of the land, my people, and Native ways.

On the wings of an eagle,
Is where I choose to be,
Where I don't have to hear the teacher lecturing me,
Up in the air, high above the trees
Feeling the air flow through my hair and into my face,
It feels so good to be here away from the world,
Looking below, I see my relatives celebrating.
They are celebrating times of joy and good times.
There is fried bread, dried fish and more,
Food from the land for everyone to share,
And necklaces for the dancers to wear.
In the center of the group, I see an elder or three,
Sitting and laughing enjoying their tea.
Telling of stories from long ago days,
Watching the child who plays,
On the wings of an eagle,
I look and imagine,
What it will be like when that down there, is me,
Having a good time enjoying my tea.
I think about how proud I am for me to be me,
A Yupik Eskimo girl in Alaska,
Who has always been taught to listen to my elders.

And to be able to dream,
And to always believe in myself,
So that I can achieve all of my goals.

Living and learning my culture and ways, to benefit me in my later days.
I enjoy dancing and listening to the stories that have to be told.
By both the people ages young and old.

On the wings of an eagle,
Is a nice place to be,
And a good way to learn your culture's history.

Death

Eddie Webb

Death: (deth), n. i. the act of dying; the end of life

Death is singing
Her gentle voice calls
me back to the beginning
of seven cycles
seven lives
seven stars
eight hundred and forty years
in human form.

Death is singing
I hear her love
I understand her purpose
I believe her song
she is coming
I fear not
my energies are focused

I will live on
with Grandmothers
and Grandfathers
Ancestors await my coming
watching me
guiding my footsteps.

Death is not dying
those are just words
Death is believing
then moving on.

RETURNING THE GIFT FESTIVAL OUTREACH PROGRAM: Writer's Workshops Student Participants

Rest No More

Marc Arthur

Me
And the night
Relaxing in the
Coming morning with some sleep.
As the sun begins to
Rise
The stars start to vanish
Hurry sun for
Under the stars I could
Rest no more.

Tanana

Willow Rose Bowen

Cool summer breezes
caress my face
I don't think I'll ever
stop loving this place

Soft rolling hills
green with endless trees
Bright rosehops and wildflowers
scattered about like leaves

With the river flowing
and the green grass blowing

As the cool summer breeze
caresses my face
I know in my heart
this place is home

Between Two Worlds

Doreen Lee Deaton

I am half Athabascan
I am half white
No culture to call my own.

Trapped between two
worlds, no culture to
call my own.

Picking up the pieces
of both worlds,
trying on the different faces, languages and customs
with no culture to
call my own.

Trapped between two worlds,
no culture to call
my own.

Him

Elizabeth Johnson

Just to feel his heart beat close to mine
 to smell the scent of his cologne
 taste the coldness of the popsicle
Just to feel the warmness of his strong hands
 to see his gorgeous face smiling at me
 hearing the warmness and comfort of his words
That's what a boyfriend is about
And what he means to me
 no one can say.
My every thoughts, dreams,
and words are of him
And always will be.
I want to know his every thought and dream
And hear the words that says he cares.
I only hope that this
 love will last forever.

Anonymously

Keith Kinzhuma

If I were a Bolt of Lightning I would strike the Earth with a sizzling Zap. I would feel the Earth hit the tip of me. I would taste the warm crisp air of the summer. I would hear the air fly past me. I would smell the ground as it burns. I would see the Earth as I fall to the earth.

The Father, Son, and Donkey

Willie Sanchez

One day these people were going to cut some wood, and they passed through the middle of one city. The son was riding on the donkey and all the people were criticizing them because the boy was on the donkey and the poor old man was walking. Then they heard the son tell his dad, "You ride the donkey and I'll walk."

But they passed through another city and the people were the same way. Then the people in the other city looked at the poor little boy walking while the man rode on the donkey. Then they passed through another city, the people were criticizing them because they are walking and the donkey was not carrying a load. Then they pass through another city and again the people were criticizing them saying, "Look the poor donkey is very tired and they are so happy riding him."

Then the father said, "Let's not listen to the people and let's do what's best for us."

Legend

Dionne Thomas

At one time there was a very rude rabbit. Rabbit always criticized all the other animals and made them feel bad. The other animals were getting tired of it. They thought if they showed him how he treated others, maybe it would change. So the next day, all the animals ignored Rabbit. If he made one bad remark to them they just turned to another direction and acted as if he wasn't there. Rabbit did not like this at all, it made him very angry. He like all of the attention he made for himself. So . . . Rabbit made a plan himself. He planned to act like he changed so that all the other animals would talk to him again. The animals liked Rabbit's new attitude, they thought he had really changed. But deep down inside all Rabbit wanted was REVENGE!

When the animals thought everything was peaceful, they went to sleep for the night. They thought since Rabbit changed, they didn't have to worry about any of his pranks. (But they were wrong.) Rabbit went to every lodge and stole everyone's food. It was during their dry season so nobody had much. This made all the animals FURIOUS! They all went to their sacred place and prayed. They asked their creator to punish Rabbit. The creator told them he would and for all the animals to act normal. That day, Rabbit lost his ability to talk.

That is why rabbits cannot talk, and are always by themselves. Just thinking of a plan of revenge! This is why everyone should treat others the way they want to be treated. If you don't something bad my happen to YOU!

WORDCRAFT CIRCLE
STUDENT PARTICIPANTS

Grandma Knows

Faith Allard

Looking at the pictures of Chugiak Mountain range of South Central Alaska reminded her of her mountain home and made her wonder how she came to be in this hot flatland of desert. Las Vegas held no comparison to Alaska, but five months ago it was a welcome change. Life had been hard for Suzie since her mother had died a year ago and now when the hardest part seemed to be over the cruel black darkness of death was at her doorstep again. This time it was Suzie. Lying in the hospital, her mind went faster than a locomotive on a midnight run but her body had stopped. She was unable to move even her eyes or her lips, yet her thoughts would not stop. The vision of her great grandmother clouded her sight until that was all she could see.

Grandmother was a tall, dark-skinned woman standing over an open pit cooking dinner for the family. Children were running and playing with sticks and dogs. A tepee was in the background and Grandma seemed to be content with her work. Suddenly she stopped and motioned for Suzie to come closer. "Sit by the fire and listen for awhile," Grandma said, pointing to the buffalo hide which was next to the fire.

Suzie sat down, just like she had when she was a child, and listened to her grandmother's soft voice explain what had happened to a girl about Suzie's age a long time ago.

"Once there was this Abenaki girl who ventured too far from the tribe," Grandma began. "The girl got lost in the woods and was gone for many days. Her tribe sent out search parties but they all came home without finding the girl. No one was able to find the young girl because she had wandered out too far to find her way back. The young girl sat on the side of a hill and cried.

One day, a turtle crawled up beside her and asked her why she had been crying. The girl told the turtle that she had been out picking berries. She told the turtle that she went too far out in the woods and now didn't know her way home. The turtle talked with her for awhile and told the girl that everything in the world had a special place to be and when things move out of their place it throws off the whole balance of life and things go wrong.

After the girl understood what the turtle was saying, she asked him if he would help her to get home. So he did, and the balance was returned." Grandma finished. "So you see, Suzie, you must go back to where you belong. You will be here soon enough. Go back to where your heart is. You can never run far enough to escape your troubles."

Grandma slowly disappeared and soon Suzie regained consciousness as she lay on the hospital bed. Suzie felt the pain of her stomach being pumped out and it felt good because she knew she was still alive. She didn't want to die. She only wanted to be with her mother and her grandmother and out of the world that had caused her so much pain.

Green Corn Song

Jesse Bruchac

We greet our mother the earth
N'wawi na wona nigawesna
from four directions
ahki wji iao

We give thanks to her
N'wlioni
for our lives
ona wjiaiak

and for the beauty
ta achi wji wlinogwak
of creation
mjassadowit

for the corn that sustains us
wji waskawanal
we sing
n'lintobna

the green corn song
ta achi . . . waskawanal lintowogan

Forty Something

Maria Dadgar

Standing in the middle of my life
I look behind and see that I have left
plenty of trailmarkers
so I can find
my way back.

I don't want to go back.
I want to blaze a new trail.
And this time I won't leave
so many markers.

The Last Great "Amventure"

Lee Francis IV

(for my father)

I would watch
as we would pass
town after town
sign after sign
watch the sun
end its journey
as we began
ours.

Hear the hum
of the engine
under my feet
the soothing vibration
of the road
as we began
our last great "amventure"
together
He and I

Soon it will be me
alone
following the sun
my dreams
continuing the legacy

Soon I will be
running the ship
playing my own music
releasing myself from the daily grind
setting out for some small town
some small motel
some well lit truck stop
where everyone looks the same

Soon it will be mine
but for now
I am content to fall asleep
with the hum of the road
and ABBA playing
in the background.

Circle

Norman E. Guardipee

Do you see that broken circle?
Do you see the charred fragments?
Put it together, put it together.
Do you see the tree of life
    withering in the middle?

Do you see the vision melting away?

Tell me if you see these things.
Tell me I'm not going crazy.

Split

Stuart Hoahwah

It's complex being a half-breed,
Being half the seed of divine balance.
Duality makes my existence Siamese twins
Seamed at the soul.
I lack Trinity's coordination of not to split.
Two planets never synchronous,
Always revolving confusion around each other.

I'm the son of the Masonic Temple,
And of Father Peyote.
Non-christian blood pulsates through my brain.
Offspring of the Calvary
And of the mysterious Quohadas,
Extinct to each other
But enemies to the last, even within me.

I hear my heritage's carbine blasts,
Moccasin retreats out of Palo Duro,
Clamor of Scottish blades and blood,
Still feeling that Celtic artillery of religion.

As my sun sets on this planetary system,
Dressing the Highlands' mythical trees in
Plaid of red and green;
Splashing into every entombed crevasse
Of the Wichita Mountains
I stand on the fence between isolation and assimilation
Balanced with a twin soul.
The empty wind picking at my Scottish plaid breechcloth

Returning the Gift

David James

Gray and heavy
like thought's early morning
movements, the clouds
hug the landscape.
Walleye, Sturgeon and Bass
watch from within the Bay,
the Lake, waiting, like lyrics.
They rise. Voices
from the trees, stones,
old mounds, broken
pottery, the stars. They rise
from ashes, bones
turned to dust,
turned again to bone,
to voice. I hear
a whisper heal
itself to song. And
ponies stomp and dance
in parking lots while
hands meet hands
and hearts touch.
And hearts heal. And
warriors of words sing
themselves whole. Warriors
sing and warriors dance
and the word is
as the word does.
We are singing ourselves
back. We are singing
ourselves home. We are
singing. We are
singing a warrior's
song. We are
singing. We are
coming home.

Noctilucent

Paul Michael Kinville

i should tell you
i wait at night

breathless

and listen
to the dark slip by

as if

i could reach my hand
behind its furry neck

and it would take me
away

to the heaven i build
in my dreams.

Come Together

Courtney Red-Horse Mohl

The eagle that soars freely
Guns that kill the thought
Mountains that come
without the thought,

A cry in the night
In the shadow of the moon
Softly turning into the wolf,

One face to the earth
All creations come together
Making peace and love.

It's Hard to Squeeze Water from a Rock

Josh Norris

It's hard to squeeze water from a rock
So for now, keep doing what you're doing.
Pounding those hallowed, hollow halls,
Placing your feet where the beat takes them.

It's hard to squeeze water from a rock
But if you listen you'll hear a song.
It may be like rain so gentle
You can't tell where it comes from
But it's as strong as a river.

It's hard to squeeze water from a rock
So when you hear that song
Chant to its beat.
Chant so loud it can never escape your soul.

It's hard to squeeze water from a rock
So let the chanting be the nourishment
That will crack the hard tile with sprouts.
Soon, the halls will deteriorate
And be replaced with a lush green meadow.

It's hard to squeeze water from a rock
So when you find yourself in that meadow
Stomp the soft earth so hard
That your voice is thrust to the heavens.
It's hard to squeeze water from a rock
So let your voice flutter and dip
Among the treetops like a flicker.

It's hard to squeeze water from a rock
So let the wind carry your voice
Until it glides and sails like an eagle.

Send your voice to the Earth
Like a gentle rain
And the People will chant your song.

Mr. Oak

Tara Charonne Picotte

There once was a very old oak tree. All of the other trees of the woods respected him for he had seen far more winters than they had.

He stood proud and tall on the western side of the woods. He was able to see the sun set every evening when the clouds allowed him to. But also he was tall enough to see it rise and this made him happy. All of the nights and days that he'd lived to see never bored him for he noticed that each day brought something different. He stood among many trees, none of which were blessed with his age. They all took care of one another.

One time he was struck by lightening and Creator must've been disappointed in him but he didn't know why. He lost his lower left branch. Actually the Creator had blessed him, for the branch had been dying from the inside. It was nature's amputation and many new healthy limbs grew to replace the other one.

His favorite season was summer time. But one other he liked was spring when he was gifted with his glory of green majesty. He provided silver-green color to the woods. He liked this time better than any other because he loved the feel of the little birds perching on his branches. And the songs they sang flowed strongly through his inner spirit.

When the summer nights began to get cooler, he knew that autumn was on its way. One morning he awoke to find that Jack Frost had made his first appearance. Now this made his roots ache with longing to still be beautiful and to be the king of this forest. But he still had another job to do before he rested.

His leaves began to float in the air. They let go to parachute down to the ground. As the days had gotten yet cooler, he lost most of his crowning glory. But his giveaway had just begun.

The acorns he'd grown since late summer were ready to fall also. And his little friends the squirrels began to feast on and store away the nuts. Oak felt glad and the squirrels were glad. Everyone was glad!

The late autumn rains began to cascade and they got colder and turned to ice. The winds got nasty cold. Soon the snow started along with the rain. Oak started to cry. The rain drops were his tear drops. He was crying because he felt useless now that winter had begun to set in. He felt isolated within himself. He'd have to look forward to the coming spring.

The night the snow began to fall, the cycle of Oak's rest started. His turn to rest had come. He went to sleep and dreams of spring filled his mind.

America The Beautiful

Lisbeth White

I am in mourning;

sweet, silent breath of eternity
clouds around me in a gray fog
dewy wet
I inhale it thickly, drawing
it shakily into my lungs, like an addict.
It weighs down my heart
but leaves me empty all the same.

And though I travel for many days
I feel like my eyes are still closed.
The fog blinds me until all the gray white-white gray
blend together with me
and I can't tell my own brown hands
from the transparent air I breathe.

I am in mourning

Lost in the cotton beard of the white man.
Lost in America
My heritage is invisible, un-distinguished.

Sometimes, behind me
I hear drums and stamping
dancing feet and
sorrowful singing
sounding like it is tugged from deep in the throat.
I smell sage burning
and sweetgrass
and I turn quickly to see nothing
but gray white-white gray
swirling around me and through me
as if I am no longer solid
as if I no longer exist.

And though I travel for many days
trying to follow the drums
I am lost
and I fear I may not be able to return
and I stumble
and I weep
and I am in mourning

Drive By

Luhui Whitebear

There went another drive by.
Another brother, gone.
Gone forever.
Never coming back.
How many more brothers?
How many more sisters?
When will we wake?
When will we see,
That's not how it should be.

Slowly we're killing each other.
Just not here,
Everywhere.
We're not the only ones.
Why do you do it?
For the thrill?
For the rush?
Does it make you feel good to know you just
    broke another heart,
    shattered another dream,
    made another relative cry?
We're the future,
But there's no future in that.

CONTRIBUTORS

SHERMAN ALEXIE (*Spokane/Coeur d'Alene*) is a remarkable poet and short story writer who has been praised for his treatment of contemporary reservation life. Sherman is the author of *The Business of Fancy Dancing*, *First Indian on the Moon*, *The Lone Ranger and Tonto Fistfight in Heaven*, and *Reservation Blues*.

FAITH ALLARD (*Sault Ste. Marie Chippewa*)is a student at Bay Mills Community College and is an emerging Native writer. Faith is a member of Wordcraft Circle.

M. COCHISE ANDERSON (*Chickasaw/Choctaw*) has had his poetry published in a wide variety of literary journals and anthologies. He currently lives in New York city.

JEANNETTE C. ARMSTRONG (*Okanagan*) is a novelist, poet, short story writer and illustrator of children's books who is known as one of the first Native women novelists in Canada. She is the author of numerous children's books and the novel, *Slash*.

CARROLL ARNETT/GOGISGI (*Cherokee*), an accomplished poet whose books of poetry include *Rounds*, *Engine*, and *Night Perimeter*. Gogisgi lives and teaches in Michigan.

MARC ARTHUR is a beginning Native student writer who participated in the Returning The Gift Outreach Program.

D. L. BIRCHFIELD (*Choctaw*) is a graduate of the University of Oklahoma College of Law. He is currently working as general editor of a ten-volume encyclopedia of American Indians.

WILLOW ROSE BOWEN, a participant in the Returning The Gift Outreach Program, she is a beginning Native student writer.

BETH BRANT (*Bay of Quinte Mohawk*), a poet, short story writer, essayist, and editor, frequently addresses her identity as a Native American, woman, and lesbian in her works. Her most recent book is *Writing As Witness: Essay and Talk*.

CHARLES BRASHEAR (*Cherokee*), an essayist, short story writer, and poet, is retired after 30 years teaching writing at three universities and is now spending his time traveling, writing, researching, and mentoring two Wordcrafters. He was recently elected as Secretary of the Wordcraft Circle's National Caucus board.

SHIRLEY BROZZO (*Chippewa*) is an emerging Native writer who was a student participant at the Returning The Gift Festival. Shirley is currently a member of Wordcraft Circle.

JAMES BRUCHAC (*Abenaki*) is the author of short stories and plays for young adults as well as articles about Abenaki culture and history. He is a member of the Dawnland Singers. James was recently elected as President of Wordcraft Circle.

JESSE BRUCHAC (*Abenaki*) is a member of Dawnland Singers. He has composed and written many of the songs on the album, *Alnobak*. A speaker of the Abenaki language, he is a student at Goddard College in Plainfield, Vermont.

JOSEPH BRUCHAC (*Abenaki*) is the author of more than thirty books of poetry, fiction, and Native American folktales and legends. He earned his doctorate from Union Graduate School in Ohio. The founding editor of the Greenfield Review Press, a respected publisher of Native American literature, he also serves on the editorial board of the journal *Studies in American Indian Literatures* and is co-editor of the *Moccasin Telegraph*, a publication of Wordcraft Circle of Native Writers & Storytellers.

BARNEY BUSH (*Shawnee/Cayuga*) is a poet and short story writer noted for works that are imbued with a sense of outrage at both past and present injustices that white society has perpetuated against Native Americans. He is the author of *My Horse and A Jukebox* and *Petroglyphs*.

E. K. (KIM) CALDWELL (*Cherokee/Shawnee*) participated in the Returning The Gift Festival on a student scholarship and is currently on the National Caucus board of Wordcraft Circle of Native Writers & Storytellers. Her writings have been published in a wide variety of journals and anthologies.

JEANETTA L. CALHOUN (*Delaware/Lenni Lenape*), a poet and reviewer who now lives in Texas.

MARIA DADGAR (*Piscataway Conoy*) is an emerging Native writer who is a student at American University and the newly elected Treasurer of Wordcraft Circle. She is an apprentice in the Wordcraft Circle Mentoring Core.

NORA DAUENHAUER (*Tlingit*) is the author with Richard Dauenhauer of *Haa Shuka, Our Ancestors* and *Haa Tuwundaaguyis*. Nora authored a book of poetry titles *The Droning Shaman*.

DOREEN LEE DEATON is a beginning Native student writer who participated in the Returning The Gift Outreach Program.

CHRISTOPHER FLEET (*Akwesasne Mohawk*), a Native poet who participated in the Returning The Gift Festival on a student scholarship, is a Wordcraft Circle member. He has served on the National Caucus board.

LEE FRANCIS (*Laguna Pueblo*) is the author of *Native Time: A Historical Time Line of Native America*. He received his Ph.D degree from Western Institute for Social Research at Berkeley, California. Currently the National Director of Wordcraft Circle of Native Writers & Storytellers, he is also the editor of *Moccasin Telegraph*.

LEE FRANCIS IV (*Laguna Pueblo*) is a member of Wordcraft Circle and is a participant in the Mentoring Core as an apprentice poet/writer. He is currently a freshman at James Madison University in Harrisonburg, Virginia.

NORMAN E. GUARDIPEE (*Blackfeet*) is a student poet who is an apprentice in Wordcraft Circle's Mentoring Core.

RUTH ANN HALL (*Hidatsa/Sioux*) participated in the Returning The Gift Festival on a Native student scholarship. She is currently a Wordcraft Circle member and is involved in the Mentoring Core as an apprentice.

LANCE HENSON (*Cheyenne*) is a poet whose verse is noted for its powerful imagery, economy of words, and universal appeal as well as its incorporation of Cheyenne philosophy and social commentary.

VI HILBERT (*Upper Skagit*) has published oral narrative and non-fiction writings in a variety of publications. She currently lives in Washington.

STUART HOAHWAH (*Comanche/Arapahoe*) is a Wordcraft Circle member who is currently attending the University of Arkansas at Little Rock. He is an active participant in the Wordcraft Circle Mentoring Core as an apprentice.

LINDA HOGAN (*Chickasaw*), a poet, short story writer, novelist, playwright, and essayist who has played a prominent role in the development of Native American poetry.

ALEX JACOBS/KARONIAKTATIE (*Mohawk*) is a freelance artist whose writings have been published in a wide variety of journals and anthologies. He is currently a Wordcraft Circle Mentor.

DAVID JAMES (*Wyandot*) is currently a graduate student at the University of Omaha. He is a member of Wordcraft Circle and participates in the Mentoring Core as an apprentice.

DONNA JOHN (*Athabascan*) participated in the Returning The Gift Festival on a student scholarship and is currently a member of Wordcraft Circle as an apprentice writer.

ELIZABETH JOHNSON was a participant in the Returning The Gift Festival Outreach Program: Writer's Workshop.

PAUL MICHAEL KINVILLE (*Sault Ste. Marie Chippewa*) is a Wordcraft Circle apprentice currently attending American University where he is majoring in English and Journalism.

KEITH KINZHUMA participated in the Returning The Gift Festival's Outreach Program: Writer's Workshop.

HAROLD LITTLEBIRD (*Laguna/Santo Domingo Pueblo*) is an established poet who has authored *On Mountain's Breath* and two tapes, *A Circle Begins* and *The Road Back In*.

RUDY MARTIN (*Tewa/Navajo/Apache*) was a poet and playwright who lived in New York city. He passed over in 1993.

KELLY MORGAN (*Lakota*) is a poet and graduate student at the University of Oklahoma who worked on the Returning The Gift Festival.

COURTNEY RED-HORSE MOHL (*Cherokee/Sioux*) is the youngest member of Wordcraft Circle who participates in the Mentoring Core as an apprentice poet.

DANIEL DAVID MOSES (*Delaware*), a poet and playwright, has been praised for his intelligent and thoughtful exploration of spiritual concerns. He is recognized for original use of imagistic language and his inclusion of Native oral traditions in his work.

JOSH NORRIS (*Yurok*) is a Wordcraft Circle member who participates in the Mentoring Core as an apprentice.

PENNY J. OLSON (*Sault Ste. Marie Chippewa*) participated in the Returning The Gift Festival on a student scholarship. She currently teaches at Bay Mills Community College and is a member of Wordcraft Circle.

ROBERT L. PEREA (*Oglala Lakota*) is a published short fiction writer who lives in Arizona. His writings have been published in a wide variety of anthologies and journals.

TARA CHARONNE PICOTTE (*Winnebago*) is a beginning poet who participated in Wordcraft Circle as an apprentice writer.

CARTER REVARD (*Osage*) is a poet, short story writer, and essayist known for verse in which he blends traditional Native images with contemporary issues and employs various poetic forms and multiple voices.

GAYLE ROSS (*Cherokee*) is an established storyteller and author. Her books include *The Girl Who Married the Moon*, *How Rabbit Trickes Otter*, and *The Story of the Milky Way*.

A. C. "CHUCK" ROSS (*Lakota*) has been in the field of education for over 23 years as a teacher, principal, superintendent, and college faculty member. He is the author of *Mitakuye Oyasin "We are all related"* and *Ehanamani "Walks Among"*.

CAROL LEE SANCHEZ (*Laguna Pueblo*) is a performing poet whose poetry and essays have been published in a wide variety of anthologies and journals. Her books of poetry include *Conversations from a Nightmare*, *Message Bringer Woman*, *excerpts from A Mountain Climber's Handbook*, and her most recent, *She) Poems*. Currently living in central Missouri where she writes and teaches, Carol Lee is a Wordcraft Circle Mentor.

WILLIE SANCHEZ was a Native student participant in the Returning The Gift Festival's Outreach Program: Writer's Workshop.

CHERYL SAVAGEAU (*Abenaki*) is an established poet and writer whose most recent book of poetry is *Home Country*. She is currently a graduate student at the University of Massachusetts Amherst and a Wordcraft Circle Mentor.

LESLIE MARMON SILKO (*Laguna Pueblo*) is a novelist, poet, and short story writer. Among the foremost writers to emerge from the Native American literary renaissance of the 1970, she is the recipient of the Lifetime Achievement Award presented by the Native Writers Circle of the Americas and the author of *Storyteller*, *Ceremony*, and *Almanac of the Dead*.

ELEANOR SIOUI (*Huron/Wyandot*) is a published poet and writer from Canada.

EVIE MICHELLE SUNNYBOY (*Yupik*) was a participant in the Returning The Gift Festival on a student scholarship.

DENISE SWEET (*White Earth Anishinabe*) is the winner of the North American Native Authors First Book Award for 1995. She is a poet who lives in Wisconsin.

DIONNE THOMAS was a Native student participant in the Returning The Gift Festival's Outreach Program: Writer's Workshop.

LINCOLN TRITT (*Gwichin Athabascan*) is a published poet from Canada.

EDDIE WEBB (*Cherokee*) was a participant in the Returning The Gift Festival on a student scholarship. He is currently a member of Wordcraft Circle and served on the National Caucus board.

LISBETH WHITE (*Mohawk/Seminole*) is a beginning writer who is an apprentice in the Mentoring Core of Wordcraft Circle.

LUHUI WHITEBEAR (*Chumash/Iroquois/Pueblo/Comanche/Huiciol*) is a beginning writer who is an apprentice in Wordcraft Circle's Mentoring Core.

ROBERTA HILL WHITEMAN (*Wisconsin Oneida*), a poet whose work has been praised for its simple and rhetorical language, vivid imagery, and sincere and distinctive voice. The is the author of *Star Quilt* and a Wordcraft Circle Mentor.

ELIZABETH WOODY (*Warm Springs/Yakima/Wasco/Navajo*) is a poet, short story writer, essayist, and visual artist whose writings are regarded as direct, deep and many-dimensional. Her artwork has been shown in galleries throughout the Northwest and in national and international touring exhibitions. She is the author of *Lumanaries of the Humble* and *Seven Hands, Seven Hearts: Prose and Poetry* and a Wordcraft Circle Mentor.

OFELIA ZEPEDA (*Tohono O'odham*) is an established writer from Arizona who has edited *When It Rains: Papago and Pima Poetry* and *The South Corner of Time*.

APPENDIX 1

Deer Hunter and White Corn Maiden

Long ago in the ancient home of the San Juan people, in a village whose ruins can be seen across the river from present-day San Juan, lived two magically gifted young people. The youth was called Deer Hunter because even as a boy, he was the only one who never returned empty-handed from the hunt. The girl, whose name was White Corn Maiden, made the finest pottery, and embroidered clothing with the most beautiful designs, of any woman in the village. These two were the handsomest couple in the village, and it was no surprise to their parents that they always sought one another's company. Seeing that they were favored by the gods, the villagers assumed that they were destined to marry.

And in time they did, and contrary to their elders' expectations, they began to spend even more time with one another. White Corn Maiden began to ignore her pottery making and embroidery, while Deer Hunter gave up hunting, at a time when he could have saved many of his people from hunger. They even began to forget their religious obligations. At the request of the pair's worried parents, the tribal elders called a council. This young couple was ignoring all the traditions by which the tribe had lived and prospered, and the people feared that angry gods might bring famine, flood, sickness, or some other disaster upon the village.

But Deer Hunter and White Corn Maiden ignored the council's pleas and drew closer together, swearing that nothing would ever part them. A sense of doom pervaded the village, even though it was late spring and all nature had unfolded in new life.

Then suddenly White Corn Maiden became ill, and within three days she died. Deer Hunter's grief had no bounds. He refused to speak or eat, preferring to keep watch beside his wife's body until she was buried early the next day.

For four days after death, every soul wanders in and around its village and seeks forgiveness from those whom it may have wronged in life. It is a time of unease for the living, since the soul may appear in the form of a wind, a disembodied voice, a dream, or even in human shape. To prevent such a visitation, the villagers go to the dead person before burial and

135

utter a soft prayer of forgiveness. And on the fourth day after death, the relatives gather to perform a ceremony releasing the soul into the spirit world, from which it will never return.

But Deer Hunter was unable to accept his wife's death. Knowing that he might see her during the four-day interlude, he began to wander around the edge of the village. Soon he drifted farther out into the fields, and it was here at sundown of the fourth day, even while his relatives were gathering for the ceremony of release, that he spotted a small fire near a clump of bushes.

Deer Hunter drew closer and found his wife, as beautiful as she was in life and dressed in all her finery, combing her long hair with a cactus brush in preparation for the last journey. He fell weeping at her feet, imploring her not to leave but to return with him to the village before the releasing rite was consummated. White Corn Maiden begged her husband to let her go, because she no longer belonged to the world of the living. Her return would anger the spirits, she said, and anyhow, soon she would no longer be beautiful, and Deer Hunter would shun her.

He brushed her pleas aside by pledging his undying love and promising that he would let nothing part them. Eventually she relented, saying that she would hold him to his promise. They entered the village just as their relatives were marching to the shrine with the food offering that would release the soul of White Corn Maiden. They were horrified when they saw her, and again they and the village elders begged Hunter to let her go. He ignored them, and an air of grim expectancy settled over the village.

The couple returned to their home, but before many days had passed, Deer Hunter noticed that his wife was beginning to have an unpleasant odor. Then he saw that her beautiful face had grown ashen and her skin dry. At first he only turned his back on her as they slept. Later he began to sit up on the roof all night, but White Corn Maiden always joined him. In time the villagers became used to the sight of Deer Hunter racing among the houses and through the fields with White Corn Maiden, now not much more than skin and bones, in hot pursuit.

Things continued in this way, until one misty morning a tall and imposing figure appeared in the small dance court at the center of the village. He was dressed in spotless white buckskin robes and carried the biggest bow anyone had ever seen. On his back was slung a great quiver with the two largest arrows anyone had ever seen. He remained standing at the center of the village and called, in a voice that carried into every home, for Deer Hunter and White Corn Maiden. Such was its authority that the couple stepped forward meekly and stood facing him.

The awe-inspiring figure told the couple that he had been sent from the spirit world because they, Deer Hunter and White Corn Maiden, had violated their people's traditions and angered the spirits; that because they had been so selfish, they had brought grief and near-disaster to the village. "Since you insist of being together," he said, "you shall have your wish. You will chase one another forever across the sky, as visible reminders that your people must live according to tradition if they are to survive." With this he set Deer Hunter on one arrow and shot him low into the western sky. Putting White Corn Maiden on the other arrow, he placed her just behind her husband.

That evening the villagers saw two new stars in the west. The first, large and very bright, began to move east across the heavens. The second, a smaller, flickering star, followed close behind. So it is to this day, according to the Tewa; the brighter one is Deer Hunter, placed there in the prime of his life. The dimmer star is White Corn Maiden, set there after she had died; yet she will forever chase her husband across the heavens.

—Translated from the Tewa by Alfonso Ortiz.

Vision : Bundle

    within   mystery wrapped in torn deer hide
      We cannot speak of the sacred
Our mother is who they want to strip : pull out her bones
      fuel their air conditioners
      unconditioned air is the one
          we breathe
          speaks to us
tongues of stars   wind   times to plant   times to be silent
They have a machine for everything   even this
one soul looking for a song we might dream
a smooth place where we could dance together
      without separation
Buttons push them
We live trapped in places we can't dig out of or move
      walls hold old voices

want to be taken down & aired   Go to a new place
No one speaks our languages
My father is ashamed of
My mother won't think
We've dead relatives & friends with no common burial place
      Scattered   they say we are vanishing
      leaves of autumn   red dust rakes away so the snow can fall flat
They have our bundles split open in museums
      our dresses & shirts at auctions
      our languages on tape
      our stories in locked rare book libraries
      our dances on film
The only part of us they can't steal
          is what we know

                by Chrystos

O Honeysuckle Woman

won't you lay with me
our tongues flowering
open-throated
golden pollen
We could drink one another
sticky sweet & deep
our bodies tracing silver snail trails
Our white teeth nibbling
We could swallow desire whole
fingers caught in our sweet smell
We'd transform the air
O honey woman
won't you suckle me
Suckling
won't you let me
honey you

              by Chrystos

I Have Not Signed a Treaty
with the U.S. Government

nor has my father nor his father
nor any grandmothers
We don't recognize these names on old sorry paper
Therefore we declare the United States a crazy person
     nightmare   lousy food   ugly clothes   bad meat
     nobody we know
No one wants to go there   This U.S. is theory   illusion
terrible ceremony   The United States can't dance   can't cook
     has no children   no elders   no relatives
They build funny houses no one lives in but papers
     Everything the United States does to everybody is bad
No this U.S. is not a good idea   We declare you terminated
     You've had your fun now go home we're tired   We signed
no treaty   WHAT are you still doing here   Go somewhere else &
     build a McDonald's   We're going to tear all this ugly mess
down now   We remove your immigration papers
     your assimilation soap suds   your stories are no good
your colors hurt our feet   our eyes are sore
     our bellies are tied in sour knots   Go Away Now
     We don't know you from anybody
You must be some ghost in the wrong place   wrong time
     Pack up your toys   garbage   lies
We   who are alive now
     have signed no treaties
Burn down your stuck houses   your sitting
     in a nowhere gray gloom   Your spell is dead
Go so far away we won't remember you ever came here
     Take these words back with you

by Chrystos

APPENDIX 2

We are the People

Grandfather	Tunka'sila
a voice I am going to send	ho uwa'yin kte
hear me	nama'hon ye
all over the universe	maka' sito/mniyan
a voice I am going to send	ho uwa'yin kte
hear me	nama'hon kte
Grandfather	Tunka'sila
I will live	wani' ktelo'
I have said it	epelo'

traditional Lakota Sioux song,
sung by Red Bird, 19th century

warrior nation trilogy

1
from the mountains we come
lifting our voices for the beautiful
road you have given

we are the buffalo people
we dwell in the light of our father sun
in the shadow of our mother earth

we are the beautiful people
we roam the great plains without fear
in our days the land has taught us oneness
we alone breathe with the rivers
we alone hear the song of the stones

2
oh ghost that follows me
find in me strength to know the wisdom
of this life

take me to the mountain of my grandfather
i have heard him all night
singing among the summer leaves

3
great spirit (maheo)

make me whole
i have come this day with my spirit
i am not afraid
for i have seen in vision
the white buffalo
grazing the frozen field
which grows near the full circle
of this
world

by Lance Henson

APPENDIX 3

Formula for Obtaining Long Life

Now, then!
Ha, now you have come to listen, you Long Human Being,
you are staying, you Helper of human beings.
You never let go your grasp from the soul.
You have taken a firmer grasp upon the soul.
I originated at the cataract, not so far away.
I will stretch out my hand to where you are.
My soul has come to bathe itself in your body.
The white foam will cling to my head as I walk
    along the path of life,
the white staff will come into my extended hand.
The fire of the hearth will be left burning for me.
The soul has been lifted up to the seventh upper world.

from the manuscript of Swimmer,
a 19th century Cherokee doctor

Long Person

Dark as wells, his eyes
tell nothing. They look
Out from the print with small regard
For this occasion.
Dressed in near black, he sits
On a folded newspaper
On a sawhorse in front of the blacksmith shop.
Wearing a black suit and white, round-brimmed hat,
My father stands on one side, his boy face
Round and serious. His brother stands
Like a reflection on the other side.
They each hold a light grasp on the edge
Of their daddy's shoulder, their fingernails
Gleaming like tiny moons on the black wool.
Each points his thumb up at the sky,
As if holding him too closely, with their whole hand,
would spur those eyes into statement.
Coming out of a depth known as dream—
Or is it memory?
I can see the door where the dim shapes
Of bellow and tongs, rings and ropes hang on the wall,
The place for fire, the floating anvil,
Snakes of railroad steel, wheels in heaps,
Piled like turtles in the dark corners.
Oconoluftee, Long Person,
You passed a stone's throw from his door,
Your ripples are Cherokee prayers.
River, Grandfather,
May your channels never break.

by Gladys Cardiff

APPENDIX 4

From My Grandmother
(1913–1970)

You were talking   to my blood
in those years before my memory
was awake. When I had no one's language
yet not Lakota not Salish
not English

You were talking me into life
and knowing. Giving me colors
the thin gray of pin feathers
on a redtail hawk for blizzard sky
I would never see. Dakota sky
just before a white out.
Your midnight blue blanket each end a light
with a mountain design yellow to red.
these were candles flames and the August night.

You were making sense of things
in image and textures
stories of Old Ones   Changers
and the Lakota I can only find
in dreams in visions.
Grandmother are we searching
out each other you and I?
Or am I just remembering
from you from my blood.

Jo Whitehorse Cochran

Old Ones Who Whisper

(The whip of the steel breeze
Ignites the thoughts
Of warm smiles from long ago.)

From a thunderous crack
A vision exposed
Glares right thru the night,

Exploding the concrete
From under your door,
I mop up the tears
Of the People who lived here before.

Understand, time is not our command
Always know, I loved U along the way
....

(And thru the glare, exposed from the night -)
the gallop of sacred stories rush the wind
the scent of burning fires
Waver like a flag unseen.

So I know who watches over
(But) it's a secret 2 me
So I ask U sister or brother
Is mine 4 U or yours 4 me?!

M. Cochise Anderson

APPENDIX 5

Telling About Coyote

Old Coyote . . .
"If he hadn't looked back
everything would have been okay
. . . like he wasn't supposed to,
                              but he did,
and as soon as he did, he lost all his power,
his strength."

". . . you know, Coyote
is in the origin and all the way
through . . . he's the cause
of the trouble, the hard times
that things have . . ."

"Yet, he came so close
to having it easy.
                    But he said,
"Things are just too easy . . ."
Of course he was mainly bragging,
shooting his mouth.
The existential Man,
Dostoevsky Coyote.

"He was on his way to Zuni
to get married on that Saturday,
and on the way there
he ran across a gambling party.
A number of other animals were there.
                    He sat in
for a while, you know, pretty sure
of himself, you know like he is,
sure that he would win something.

                     But he lost
everything. Everything.
And that included his skin, his fur
which was the subject of envy
of all the other animals around.
Coyote had the prettiest,
the glossiest, the softest fur
that ever was. And he lost that.

                     So some mice
finding him shivering in the cold
beside a rock felt sorry for him.
"This poor thing, beloved,"
they said, and they got together
just some old scraps of fur
and glued them on Coyote with pinon pitch.
And he's had that motley fur every since.
You know, the one that looks like
scraps of an old coat, that one."

Coyote, old man, wanderer,
where you going, man?
Look up and see the sun.
Scorned, an old raggy blanket
at the back of the closet nobody wants.

"At this one conference
of all the animals there was a bird
with the purest white feathers.
His feathers were like, ah . . .
like the sun was shining on it
all the time but you could look at it
and you wouldn't be hurt by the glare.
It was easy and gentle to look at.
And he was Crow.
He was sitting at one side of the fire.
And the fire was being fed large pine logs,
and Crow was sitting downwind
from the fire, and the wind was blowing
that way . . .

And Coyote was there.
He was envious of Crow because
all the other animals were saying,
"Wowee, look at that Crow, man,
just look at him," admiring Crow.
Coyote began to scheme.
He kept throwing pine logs into the fire,
ones with lots of pitch in them.
And the wind kept blowing.
all night long . . .
Let's see,
the conference was about deciding
the seasons—when they should take place—
and it took a long time to decide that . . .
And when it was over, Crow was covered
entirely in soot. The blackest soot
from the pine logs.
And he's been like that since then."
"Oh yes, that was the conference
when Winter was decided
that it should take place
when Dog's hair got long.
Dog said,
"I think Winter should take place
when my hair gets long."
And it agreed that it would. I guess
no one else offered a better reason."

Who?
Coyote?

O,
O yes, last time . . .
when was it,
I saw him somewhere
between Muskogee and Tulsa,
heading for Tulsy Town I guess,
just trucking along.
He was heading into some oakbrush thicket,
just over the hill was a creek.

Probably get to Tulsa in a couple of days,
drink a little wine,
tease with the Pawnee babes,
sleep beside the Arkansas River,
listen to the river move,
. . . hope it don't rain,
hope the river don't rise.
He'll be back Don't worry.
He'll be back.

Simon Ortiz

Broken Tradition

As I walked through the park one day
I saw a young man sitting on the grass
beside a tree, playing a guitar.

A dead squirrel lay beside him.
I walked up to him, looked at the squirrel
"What happened?" I asked the young man.
He looked at me.

"I don't know," he said.
"I was just sitting here, playing my guitar,
and . . . plop!
and squirrel's laying there . . . dead beside me."

I looked around the park.
I watched the other squirrels.
This is what I surmised.
Squirrel had broken "TRADITION".

Instead of hunting for berries and nuts,
he went begging for "junk food"
Candy, popcorn, etc.
he was showing off.

He climbed up too high in the tree,
go sick, fell out of the tree.
Broke his neck . . .
"Tsk-tsk . . . Brother Squirrel"

Shoulda stuck to Tradition.

Vince Wannassay

APPENDIX 6

Remember

Remember the sky that you were born under,
know each of the star's stories.
Remember the moon, know who she is. I met her
in a bar once in Iowa City.
Remember the sun's birth at dawn, that is the
strongest point of time. Remember sundown
and the giving away to night.
Remember your birth, how your mother struggled
to give you form and breath. You are evidence of
her life, and her mother's and hers.
Remember your father. He is your life, also.
Remember the earth whose skin you are:
red earth, black earth, yellow earth, white earth
brown earth, we are earth.
Remember the plants, trees, animal life who all have their
tribes, their families, their histories, too. Talk to them,
listen to them. They are alive poems.
Remember the wind. Remember her voice. She knows the
origin of this universe. I heard her singing Kiowa war
dance songs at the corner of Fourth and Central once.
Remember that you are all people and that all people
are you.
Remember that you are this universe and that this
universe is you.
Remember that all is in motion, is growing, is you.
Remember that language comes from this.
Remember the dance that language is, that life is.
Remember.

Joy Harjo

APPENDIX 7

Heritage

From my mother, the antique mirror
where I watch my face take on her lines.
She left me the smell of baking bread
to warm fine hairs in my nostrils,
she left the large white breasts that weigh down
my body.

From my father I take his brown eyes,
the plague of locusts that leveled our crops,
they flew in formation like buzzards.

From my uncle the whittled wood
that rattles like bones
and is white
and smells like all our old houses
that are no longer there. He was the man
who sang old chants to me, the words
my father was told not to remember.

From my grandfather who never spoke
I learned to fear silence.
I learned to kill a snake
when you're begging for rain.

And grandmother, blue-eyed woman
whose skin was brown,
she used snuff.
When her coffee can full of black saliva
spilled on me
it was like the brown cloud of grasshoppers
that leveled her fields.
It was the brown stain
that covered my white shirt,

my whiteness a shame.
That sweet, black liquid like the food
she chewed up and spit into my father's mouth
when he was an infant.
It was the brown earth of Oklahoma
stained with oil.
She said tobacco would purge your body of poisons.
It has more medicine than stones and knives
against your enemies.

That tobacco is the dark night that covers me.

She said it is wise to eat the flesh of deer
so you will be swift and travel over many miles.
She told me how our tribe has always followed a stick
that pointed west
that pointed east.
From my family I have learned the secrets
of never having a home.

Linda Hogan